SUMMARY

Cornish hedges are often 2500-5000 ? flowering species per mile. Being the n̲ ̲ ̲ ̲ ̲ ̲ ̲ ̲ ̲ ̲ ̲ ̲ ̲ ̲ ̲ ̲ ̲ ̲ ̲ ̲, they are a valuable tourism asset. They differ from English thorn hedges, being generally built stone-faced with a subsoil core. Many incomers to Cornwall need to understand the care of our hedges. The Guidance Note gives the required action.

Annual spring and summer close-trimming of hedges soon causes a catastrophic decline in two-thirds of the different plant species, and this alters the look of the landscape. Wildlife species may be self-sustaining in hedges, or non-sustaining and rely on nearby habitats. Fortunately most species recover when hedges are trimmed once every few years, and then only during winter months. Trimming less close to the hedge and the use of protective wire for most hedges improves the habitat, preserves the hedge structure and is cheaper for the farmer.

An untilled field margin increases the hedgerow wildlife, and helps to protect field crops and hedge structure.

Trees soon re-appear in the landscape if the top-cuts along the hedge are correctly angled. Traditional coppicing of hedgerow trees preserves them and the hedge structure.

Use of proposed categories of roadside hedges can double the roadside plant species.

Instructions are given for achieving the aims of the Cornwall County Council's Environmental Charter.

ACKNOWLEDGEMENTS

The author is indebted to Mr Down, who learnt his hedging skills in the 1880s, for showing him many of them 50 years ago, and to many farmers and workers since. The booklet is only possible with Sarah Carter's unique study of the same 2 miles of roadside Cornish hedge during the last 34 years, and with the encouragement and help given by the staff at the Cornish Biological Records Unit and other local conservationists. Thanks are also due to E.C.M. Haes, B. Roskilly and Messrs Teagle for their illustrations, and to the Cornwall Archaeological Unit for historical information. The cover pictures are by Sarah Carter who has also helped with the editing.

THE AUTHOR

The Cornish hedge is as much an integral part of our natural wildlife as of our ancient history and beautiful landscape. Not always appreciated is that it is distinctly different from the English hedgerow and upland drystone wall.

This booklet by Robin Menneer is a direct response to this misunderstanding and fills a long-felt need to describe the value of typical Cornish hedges which are richer in wildlife than their counterparts east of the Tamar. More than that, he explains how with careful management of the often exuberant vegetation, the ancient structure of a hedge can be preserved and its wildlife diversity increased. Loss of tradition and recent changes in farming have combined to reduce the wildlife and landscape value of the Cornish countryside. This booklet seeks to reverse this trend by setting out practical ways of restoring the Cornish hedge to its former glory. The text and illustrations have been prepared free of cost in the interests of Cornish wildlife.

I am very pleased to be associated with this work and its author, Robin Menneer, son of a Cornish farmer, who learnt hedging 50 years ago from a traditional hedger. He has had a lifetime of involvement with farmers and farming practices, through MAFF and rural conservation, including setting up and running the West Penwith Environmentally Sensitive Area.

This book contains material for a wide readership. Newcomers to Cornwall will find help in understanding how wildlife in Cornish hedges is not only preserved but revived. Whether experienced in farming or a beginner to cultivation, the reader will find vital information, and there is sound advice for those of us lucky enough to have a Cornish hedge bounding our garden. Wildlife enthusiasts will be persuaded to take a fresh look at our hedges as uniquely diversified habitats.

Stella Treharne Turk
Hon. Research Fellow
Cornish Biological Records Unit
Institute of Cornish Studies (University of Exeter)
Pool, Redruth.

THE GUIDANCE NOTE FOR WILDLIFE REVIVAL IN CORNISH HEDGES

1. Hedges, apart from roadside hedges, should be trimmed at intervals of not less than 3-5 years, the number of years depending on growth, and trimmed only between the start of November and the end of February, extended to October and March on wet ground.

2. Hedges should be trimmed quickly so as to leave about 250mm-500mm (12"-20") of growth on each side. Hedge tops should never be cut square, but should be trimmed at a slanting angle of 60° leaving a centre strip 0.5-1m ($^1/_2$-1yd) wide for scrub and stooled tree growth. Growth on hedge tops should be traditionally coppiced or cut-and-laid depending on the local circumstance.

3. If the underlying structure of a hedge cannot economically be made stockproof, the hedge should first be trimmed especially close to allow a permanent fence to be set hard against the stone or turf of the hedge. Subsequently the hedge is trimmed against the wire. Other specified wiring methods should be used in appropriate conditions,.

4. Growing trees should be coppiced traditionally when trunks exceed 250mm (10") diameter at 1.2m (4') high: "As thick as a man's thigh at breast height." Over-mature trees should be shortened to a tall stump before becoming liable to windblow.

5. The underlying hedge structure, including stiles, should be maintained in the manner traditional to the locality.

6. Regard should be given to farming policy, and to the locality and structure of each hedge.

7. Nearby habitats should be kept. A wildlife field margin 1-2m (1-2 yds) wide should be unsprayed, unfertilized and topped annually.

8. Hedge growth should not be controlled routinely by herbicide. The contamination of hedges from spray drift and inaccurate fertiliser spreading should be avoided.

9. Heavy infestation by rabbits should be avoided.

10. Roadside hedges should be trimmed in accordamce with the specified catagories agreed with the Cornwall County Council.

CONTENTS

                                                                                                        Page

The Guidance Note for Wildlife Revival in Cornish Hedges

Chapter:

1.	History of Cornish Hedges	6
2.	Hedges in the Cornish Landscape	9
3.	WIldlife Importance of Cornish Hedges	11
4.	Traditional Hedge Structures in Cornwall	22
5.	Effects of Recent Farming Changes on Traditional Cornish Hedges	26
6.	Methods of Trimming Cornish Hedges	30
7.	Close and Off-set Wire Fences	36
8.	Wildlife Field Margins	41
9.	Treatment of Hedgerow Trees	49
10.	Control of Rabbits in Cornish Hedges	55
11.	Roadside Hedges, Legal Obligations & Special Needs	57

References and Appendices

1.

HISTORY OF CORNISH HEDGES.

Dating early British farming is inexact, but many Cornish hedges are older than most in other parts of Britain. Much archaeological evidence has been found recently by the Cornwall Archaeology Unit, though not enough to dispel a degree of conjecture.

During the Mesolithic period, about 7000 BC to 4000 BC, Cornwall was generally wooded, with locally-made flint axes being used for felling trees for the limited needs of a primitive agricultural community. In the late-Neolithic period 4000-2000 BC (the age of Stonehenge) nomadic husbandry of cattle and sheep became more skilled, and slash-and-burn cultivation expanded. Fields were first created for cereal crops during the late-Neolithic Age and enclosed by the first Cornish hedges. This period overlapped into the Bronze Age, 2500-500 BC, during which there was an increase in population and change in Cornish landscapes, due to the mining and smelting of metals, similar to the changes of the later Industrial Revolution elsewhere. Clearance of woodland for the tin and copper mining industry was linked with the food needs of the non-agrarian population, and led to conversion into farmland. With a local economy rich from mining, there were adequate resources for this agricultural expansion to take place.

Prehistoric farms were about 5 to 10 hectares (12 - 25 acres) with extended-family homesteads about a half-mile apart with rough land, usually lowland heath but often scrub or wetland, separating each holding from its neighbour. The typical size of a Bronze Age field was about 0.1 hectare ($^1/_2$ acre), 25 to 35 metres square, ideal for hand tillage. Lines of the original hedges made convenient use of large surface boulders and the lie of the land, often causing kinks in the hedge and lynchets (topsoil drifts uphill of hedges). Thus the first fields were enclosed, grazed with animals, cultivated and sown with cereals in rotation.

Figures 1 and 2 illustrate some of the present field enclosures near Zennor in West Cornwall. Even the field sizes in Figure 1 follow some 2000 years of amalgamation of the original tiny fields. With intervening hedges removed to make larger fields, these Bronze Age curvilinear hedges now appear to meander sinuously across the landscape. Figure 2 depicts existing field boundaries a mile distant from those in Fig.1, with later hedges, built during the thousand years following the arrival of the Celts in about 600 BC, showing an obvious straightness in the countryside.

Figure 1

0.7 ha
1.0 ha
0.5 ha
0.4 ha
0.4 ha
0.4 ha

Existing Bronze Age fields

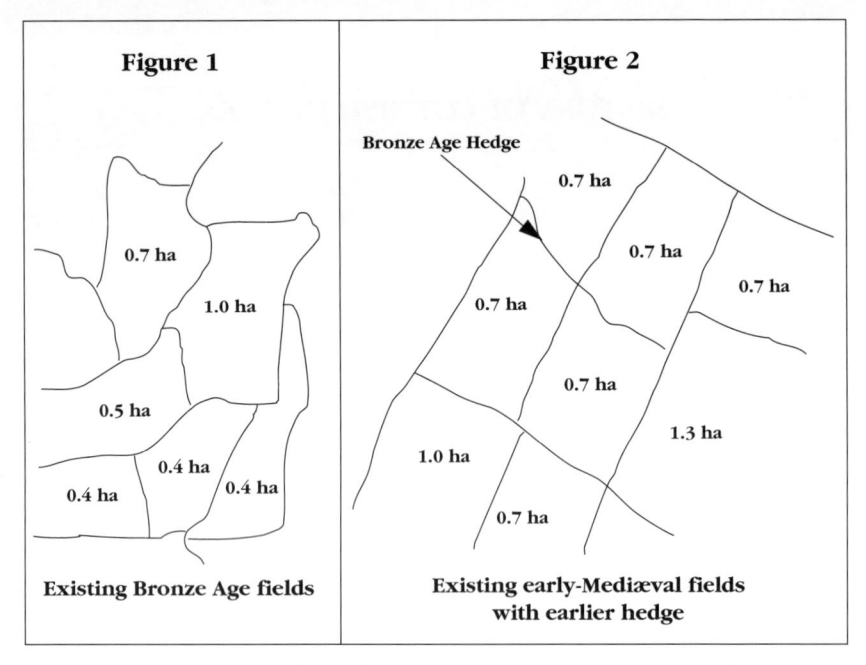

Figure 2

Bronze Age Hedge
0.7 ha
0.7 ha
0.7 ha
0.7 ha
0.7 ha
1.0 ha
1.3 ha
0.7 ha

Existing early-Mediæval fields with earlier hedge

Figure 2 also shows how the older Bronze Age curvilinear hedge was incorporated when the fields were 'rationalised' probably 500 to 1000 years ago.

Large landed estates originated with annexation by the Saxons and Normans, often with absentee landlords. The Mediæval open-field system was not generally imposed upon the Cornish who continued with their self-contained holdings.

There were few, if any, Enclosure Act awards in Cornwall because the easily tillable land was already enclosed. In the early years of the 19th century, Worgan (1811) writing for the Board of Agriculture observed: "However, of late years, some farms have been considerably extended, by enclosing many acres of the wastes contiguous thereto, with good substantial stone, or turf hedges, for permanent improvement". This was land that had been cultivated 2000 years earlier and left to waste, but the Napoleonic naval blockade was almost as serious as during the last war when moorland re-enclosure was again encouraged.

The mining industry has always alternated between boom and slump, and many miners kept small farms or gardens on which they relied for food during times of depression. This tended to preserve many old field boundaries, though until 150 years ago the profits to farmers from trading with the mining industry provided extra money for the progressive farmer to enlarge his fields and straighten out his hedges. These later hedges tend to enclose fields of 1 to 2 hectares (2 - 5 acres).

Of particular local interest are the Early Mediæval Oak woods, often estuarine, used until this century to produce charcoal for tin smelting and bark for 'cutching' nets and tanning leather to equip the immense equine transport system required for the mining industry. Because these trees were coppiced on a 60 or so year cycle, most of them are many centuries old.

The keeping of traditional countryside practices by the Cornish over the centuries has preserved many of the habitats lost during farming changes in other parts of Britain. Our hedges provide vital connecting stepping-stones for the relevant wildlife.

Some of the older hedges have had their damage by livestock repaired as they occured over the millennia without any apparent alteration of hedging style. Many of these hedges run along the contours and have accumulated washed-down topsoil on their uphill sides, often to a depth of 1-2m (1-2yds), forming lynchettes. Each of these contains, layer by layer, an accumulation of the past and, although unlikely to harbour gold treasure, is a rich repository of scientific information which we are only now beginning to be able to unraffle.

Other old hedges have been taken down and re-built along the original line but in a different style (see photograph).

New hedges are being built which, after a few years, appear to the layman to be ancient. These can be usually indentified by the lack of weathering of the stone and by the plant species growing in the hedge.

So the age of any particular hedge cannot easily be assumed.

Wild Madder and Polypody Fern

2.

HEDGES IN THE CORNISH LANDSCAPE

In 1994, one-quarter of Cornwall was scheduled as an Area of Outstanding Natural Beauty. The Cornish hedge is the most prominent linear feature in the Cornish landscape, estimated at about 30,000±20% miles (T.Edwards, personal communication) and equivalent to an area about the size of Penwith west of Penzance. Around the coast, Cornish hedges often provide granitic landscape links between outcropping rock on the high land and the craggy sea cliffs. Cornwall, a richly dissected series of plateaux rising to a central granite spine, would be bare and uninteresting if deprived of the apparently random field divisions provided by unkempt woody hedges. This is already evidenced where over-enthusiastic annual trimming has reduced the hedges to the monotonous urbanised appearance of tidy town hedges, as shown in the same view on the front and back covers of this book. Misguided maintenance also blurs the different visual effects that the many different styles of hedge have across Cornwall. Revival of the flowering plants and trees in the hedges will do much to restore our landscape.

"Untidy Cornish hedges are a precious asset in our villages and countryside."

The traditional hedges in Cornwall with their undulating floral and tree cover are a significant tourist attraction which has too often been taken for granted. The patchwork of our fields is a feature of the landscape which is cherished beyond our shores and, like other elements of our heritage, needs to be appreciated by us, rather than merely accepted (Maclean, 1992). From a distance it is perhaps the variety afforded to the eye by hedge and hedgerow tree that is their greatest asset, while close at hand it is the scents, sights and sounds of the inhabitant plants and animals that has endeared them to the naturalist and the public at large (Fry & Lonsdale, 1991). Their gradual deterioration over the past 50 years due to lapse of tradition has been parallelled elsewhere in Britain where widespread removal has led to an open prairie-like landscape. Nearby rough land and woods augment hedge wildlife as well as being an integral visual feature.

Whilst hedges still have a role to play in commercial agriculture, this is much less than in the centuries before winter stock-housing and large farm machinery. Farming structure has also altered because bigger farms are keeping herds of cattle with increased propensity to find weaker sections of field hedges. Unfortunately, changes in farming practice may, over several years, reduce a good Cornish hedge to little more than a rough scar across the landscape unless there is appropriate action by the farmer.

2.1 Hedges not on Farms

Numerous hedges are owned by non-farmers, especially those around dwelling-houses. Here is an opportunity for good traditional maintenance using hook and slasher, or electric hedge trimmer, rather than the strimmer or herbicide (see Chapter 6). The wish to display the stone facing of Cornish hedges, or to trim during early or mid summer, has to be firmly resisted, as these methods have a disastrous effect on species and can ultimately cause a collapse of the hedge structure by erosion.

Properly conserved as a wildlife habitat, Cornish hedges in villages are much more rewarding than the planted hedge or concrete block wall which often replaces them. Those few Cornish hedges surviving within towns are especially precious and are the more deserving of traditional management.

Local authority planning departments are now exerting more pressure on developers to retain or replace Cornish hedges. Regrettably the new hedges are usually less substantial than those nearby, and are built erroneously with a topsoil core. Too often, if the new hedge is on an industrial site, aggressive neglect occurs. In public municipal areas it may become an object of gradual demolition by the local youngsters. Only on farms are new hedges cared for by proper hedgers; most of the time by the farmer himself.

Wren and Wolf Spider

3.

WILDLIFE IMPORTANCE OF CORNISH HEDGES

(Latin names of plants are given in the appendices and follow Stace, 1990)

The hedge is a man-made structure of recent emergence in evolutionary terms. No new species have evolved to occupy this new habitat, but the wide variety of combinations of stone, soil type and aspect in hedges across Cornwall has resulted, over the millennia, in colonisation from woodland, scrub, moorland, cliff and grassland. Many species in Cornish hedges are refugees from habitats long vanished.

The original wildlife habitats in Cornwall were reduced as prehistoric man started to cultivate his fields, but within the cultivated parts we put up our Cornish hedges, at first a dense network enclosing very small fields, which acted as refuges for those species which could cope with this new hedge environment. Gradually as the cultivated land spread and the fields got bigger, the number and size of areas of original habitat shrank. In many locations the original environment has gone altogether, leaving the wildlife to survive on the hedges. These may be termed 'self-sustaining species'.

In many other places, there are areas of original habitat, albeit evolving, which sustain their own variety of wildlife. From these nucleus habitats, wildlife spreads out into the surrounding countryside via the hedges. For many species the hedge is not their preferred habitat, and some rely in the long term on the original habitat for sustaining their population in hard times, i.e. they are 'non-sustaining species'. Even so, in normal times the hedges surrounding a nucleus habitat are likely to have total numbers within some species many times greater than in the original area. Importantly these non-sustaining species increase the variety of wildlife in the hedges.

For example, hedges surrounding a small heathland usually contain some plant and animal species which will remain in those hedges as long as the heathland remains (non-sustaining species); but those hedges also host plants and animals which, while originating in the heathland, are able to survive indefinitely in the hedge as a substitute habitat (self-sustaining species).

The overall abundance of plant species in Cornish hedges is related to the warm winters and summers without many droughts. Cornwall enjoys a low latitude combined with the influence of the North Atlantic Drift and has a maritime climate providing frequent opportunities throughout the year for seed germination. In plant distribution, a well-maintained Cornish hedge often resembles a vertical flower-meadow, as opposed to an ordinary thorn hedge which may approximate to linear woodland (Mrs M Combe, pers. comm.).

The wide diversity of plant species is also because many are likely to have existed uninterrupted for 6000 years in the earlier hedges. As hedges age, the probability of new arrivals establishing themselves lessens with the reduction of vacant ecological niches and, in unchanging circumstances over the centuries, one might expect a loss of diversity. But, as described below, the general habitat of the Cornish hedge alters with its treatment, for better or worse.

Elements of the original woodland, e.g. Dog's Mercury, Wood Anemone and Bluebell, persist in many hedges in Cornwall. Studies of old woods have shown that Dog's Mercury normally spreads at only 200mm (8") a year (Pollard et al., 1974), yet it is in many Cornish hedges. The collapse of the copper and tin mining resulted in mass emigration. Some hedge plants, e.g. Mexican Fleabane, have been associated with 'Cousin Jacks' returning from metalliferous mining in the New World.

3.1 Number of Species

The Cornish Biological Records Unit (CBRU) maintains the computerised database for wildlife in Cornwall. Its check-list of Cornish hedge species contained 75,000 records in September 1992. The hedge check-list totals 872 species and subspecies of plants and ferns, of which 518 are native, 32 being Scarce and 13 listed in the Red Data Book (1983). There are over 80 trees and shrubs recorded. Most of these plant species are self-sustaining, others (non-sustaining) rely on nearby rough land, cliffs, woods etc., to recolonise hedges following population crashes.

Because of Cornwall's climate, maritime trade and tradition of exotic great gardens, the total of 354 introduced species is not surprising, though the merit of their preservation is controversial. Most exotic plants are ordinary garden escapes, regrettably many spread into the wild by misguided gardeners e.g. Japanese Knotweed.

3.2 Plants

The earliest written record of a named plant in Cornwall was by M de Lobel in 1576, the first British note of the Barren Strawberry which is often found in our hedges (Hamilton Davey, 1909). The flora of Cornish hedges has been described more recently by Paton (1968). Keble

Martin's index (1965) of botanical names in his Concise British Flora amounts to about 2500. The Nature Conservancy Council in 1970 described 250 flowering plants and ferns as being recorded from hedges in Britain. It seems clear that while sites of hedge species may still be regionally under-recorded for the whole of Britain, hedges in Cornwall contain more species than those in other parts of Britain, and a significant proportion of the total plant species occurring in Britain. The same can be said for lichens and mosses (Paton, 1969).

Coincidentally two surveys were made independently near Penzance and Camborne, in each case taking a random length of about one mile of country lane. The recorded results (Carter, 1985, 1986 and Murphy, 1985) showed that both had found in excess of 160 different plant species in their hedges, described further in Chapter 3.5. The Women's Institute recorded 168 plant species in a survey of 10 yd stretches of hedges throughout Cornwall in 1975, a drought year, finding half the hedges uncut (Bere, 1982).

Some plants are in flower in the Cornish hedge throughout the year. A count by Mrs S. Gartside (pers. comm. 1993) of wild flowering plants within 5 miles of her home in West Cornwall, during the first week in January 1993, yielded some 46 plants actually in flower, of which 33 were in hedges.

In less prosperous days, the hedgerow harvest of blackberries every autumn was the mainstay of puddings for many winter days, Elder flowers and berries were the basis of many old remedies, sloes for festive sloe gin and, as the author remembers, the leaves of Common Sorrel (Sour-sabs) to assuage thirst when walking home from school.

Most of the British tree species are represented in Cornish hedges, together with many exotics planted during and after the years of mining prosperity. Hedgerow trees host many animals and are important in providing a variable and dappled shade for the plants underneath. The more frequently occurring 'native' broadleaf trees are the Sycamore, Ash, Elm var. and Sessile Oak. Elm perpetuates itself by suckers, now fast recovering after Dutch Elm disease but badly handicapped by the over-severe hedge trimming. In Cornwall, Elm, Ash and Sycamore regenerate readily from live stumps (stool growth), Oak to a lesser extent. Ash and Sycamore have wind-dispersed seeds also small enough to be carried by many birds, so have few problems in colonising Cornish hedges. Oak relies more on woodland rodents and the Jay for its distribution, so needs human help if many of our hedges are again to harbour the 500-600 species associated with oaks (Appendix E). A relinking of the many woods, by way of oaks in hedges, would do much to counteract the fragility of smaller oak-related habitats.

3.3 Animals

In the mild but windy and exposed conditions that prevail across much of Cornwall, the still extensive hedges provide what is often the only effective shelter for many invertebrate species, particularly flying insects. Hedges are the 'stepping-stones' which enable insects to move from one habitat to another (Fry & Lonsdale, 1991), but some will stay and breed temporarily on non-preferred foodplants. In many areas the varied terrain in the immediate vicinity of a hedge may be the only place where key vegetation and food chains supporting necessarily self-sustaining local species may be found (E.C.M. Haes, pers. comm.). Of special significance are the many narrow green lanes developed for pack-animal trains serving the mines. Generally these are too narrow for road traffic, and where they are not over-grown they provide a perfect wind-free sun-trap for invertebrates, conspicuously butterflies.

All British reptiles, 40% of mammal species, 20% of birds, 42% of butterflies and 47% of bumble-bees live in hedges and roadside verges in Britain (Bere, 1982); and it is anticipated that much higher proportions are likely to be found in the more diverse Cornish hedges and verges.

Humphreys (1980) recorded, in his 32 km^2 survey at St. Ives, 21 species of land mollusca in 9 diverse habitats, including sand dunes. He found that 16 of these 21 species were in Cornish hedges, 2 more than those in both woodland and scrub combined, indicating the diversity of the mainly non-calcareous hedge habitats.

Of the 25 species of bumblebees recorded in the British Isles, 22 (88%) have been recorded in Cornwall (Almond, 1975). The varied rough vegetation and mossy areas of the freely-draining sides and tops of traditional Cornish hedges provide probably the majority of their nest sites.

The families of shield bugs, lacewings etc. are well represented in Cornwall, with 277 (55%) species recorded (CBRU) out of the British total of 507 species. They are roughly the size of a human finger nail and their solid shape and beautiful, sometimes metallic, colouring, as well as their resonant buzz as they launch into their clumsy flight, suggest beings from a warmer climate. They flourish particularly well in Cornish hedges, most suck sap from plants but some eat caterpillars and similar soft prey (E.C.M. Haes, pers. comm.).

The complex habitat of Cornish hedges is rich in beetles, including Glow-worms seen in evenings during the summer and whose larvae feed on tiny snails. Of much interest are the tiny flea beetles, crimson with brilliant blue wing cases, the curiously shaped tortoise beetles and a group which suggest outsized ladybirds. Where bedstraw plants are common, the large matt-black Bloody-nosed Beetle is often seen (E.C.M. Haes, pers. comm.). A. Spalding, (pers. comm.) recorded 28 species of beetle (including three nationally notable species) in an 820m (900 yds) section of hedgerow in north Cornwall. The recording was done on a day in July 1989 by shaking the beetles into a beating tray. The hedgerow was a typical Cornish hedge about 2m (8') high, with a mix of shrubby species such as Hawthorn and Blackthorn and small trees such as Oak and Ash. It is likely that older and larger hedgerows may contain a larger number of beetle species.

Recorded in the Cornish Biological Records Unit are 169 (66%) of the 256 species of Hoverflies in Britain (Stubbs & Falk, 1983). Even a short 84m length of hedge was found by Barker (1986) to contain about 30 of the more conspicuous species of hoverfly. Some of these are the neatly striped black-and-yellow flies, often mistaken for wasps, which prey on aphids during the summer.

Bush-crickets, mainly the Great Green Bush-cricket and the Dark Bush-cricket, are numerous in Cornish hedges, and their evening chorus produced by stridulation brings a reminder of the Mediterranean cicadas to our tourists resorts. About 200 Bush-crickets were counted during the first week of August 1990 in a quarter-mile length of roadside hedge near Hayle. Both these species thrive in the cover of lightly trimmed hedges, which provide adequate food for their omnivorous appetites (E.C.M. Haes, pers. comm.).

Dragonflies are aquatic as nymphs but, when adult, need to feed on insects for a week or so before returning to the waterside to mate. In Cornwall the sunny sides of the hedges provide an excellent non-sustaining habitat. Four of the larger hawkers are frequently seen, including the Emperor Dragonfly, our largest native species (E.C.M. Haes, pers comm).

There are 14 species of Butterfly (Appendix D) associated with Cornish hedges. These are more than one-third of the total Cornish species and are capable of sustaining their populations totally within the hedgerow habitat. There are possibly another dozen non-sustaining species that visit hedges, or will breed there temporarily when they have a permanent habitat close by from which replacements come after a poor season (Appendix B). Our traditionally managed hedges provide the mixture of sun and shade beloved of both woodland and meadow species. Their requirements include nectar and shelter for adults and suitable foodplants for their caterpillars. Bramble blossom is especially attractive to adult butterflies which frequently establish and guard territories even though their caterpillars may live elsewhere. Farm lanes with a traditionally managed hedge on each side are especially valuable. (A. Spalding, pers. comm.).

About 150 species of the larger moths are usually self-sustaining in association with Cornish hedges (Appendix E). Carter observed that caterpillars feed on about 100 of the 180 hedge species of plants and on about 70 of the 150 field species listed in Appendices A and C. Many moth species use a very wide variety of food plants; caterpillars of the Silver Y moth, for instance, have been recorded on 220 different species in 51 plant families (Novák, 1985). Many are eaten as substitutes mainly when the preferred plant is not available, others by non-sustaining species which visit or breed temporarily, and by the smaller moth species.

Insects from a wide variety of larval habitats depend on pollen or nectar in their adult stages and these food sources are provided year-round in Cornwall by the wide variety of hedgerow plants with their different flowering seasons. The flowers of the thorns and willows attract a profusion of insects early in the year, while the combined flowering of the various members of the Umbelliferae e.g. Cow Parsley and Hogweed, of the Compositae e.g. Ox-eye Daisy and Ragwort and of the Labiatae e.g. Woundwort and Betony, means that pollen and nectar are plentiful from March to November; flowers are present throughout the winter (Mrs S. Gartside, pers. comm.). An additional sugar source for some insects is honeydew excreted by aphids.

Our native reptiles Adder, Grass Snake, Slow-worm and Common Lizard require open vegetation providing cover at ground level with easy access to sunlight for basking. Suitable management of the south face of hedges is crucial. Bare stones here-and-there are useful as they retain heat; these are particularly used by the Common Lizard, which is the most agile species. The base of the hedge, and the verge next to it, are important basking, hunting and sheltering sites for all species and an open vegetation structure needs to be maintained (M. Nicholson, Cornwall Trust for Nature Conservation, CTNC, pers. comm.). This requires the mosaic of uneven-aged plants in the dry lowland less-fertile habitat typical of traditional Cornish hedges.

Traditionally-kept hedges provide food, shelter, nesting sites and song perches for many bird species. The number of species is related to the size of the hedge, the amount of scrub on its sides and top and to the diversity of trees. Although hedges may not be the preferred and original habitat type, many birds are self-sustaining in our traditionally managed hedges. Those species originating in woodland (eg Chaffinch, Great Tit) need tree growth. The scrub and the trimmed sides attract the woodland margin and scrub species (eg Dunnock, Whitethroat). Hedges devoid of scrub attract few birds (McCartney, 1993). On the Lizard a survey of breeding birds by Pay (1993) recorded a rich diversity of habitats in a sheltered area of traditional hedges. It held good populations of Wren, Dunnock, and Robin and, along timbered stretches, Blue Tit. The Chaffinch was also abundant provided there were elevated perches from which to sing. In addition the traditional hedges provided nest-sites for Greenfinch and Goldfinch. Whitethroat preferred thick shrub cover around the base of the hedges. The approximate numbers of breeding pairs in hedges is relevant: Wren about 50/km^2, Dunnock, Chaffinch and Robin 30/km^2, Blue Tit 20/km^2, Whitethroat, Greenfinch and Great Tit 5-10/km^2, Bullfinch, Linnet, Goldfinch, Chiffchaff and Willow Warbler 2-5/km^2. The density of most of these species is well in excess of the national average breeding densities (which include woodland areas and therefore more apparent diversity). Notably some hedges in a small part of this Lizard survey had been trimmed too often and too tight; this area was conspicuously devoid of breeding birds. In exposed open countryside, a typical victim of hedge mismanagement is the Yellow Hammer, easily recognised by its song "a little bit of bread and no cheese", the catastrophic decline of which has been aided by elimination of the bushes and trees from which the males sing. Other birds, roosting and nesting elsewhere, use hedges as feeding grounds, and they suffer from the loss of seeds and insects along over-trimmed hedgesides.

Mammals, including the ubiquitous rabbit, make use of the Cornish hedge. It is the self-sustaining home of mice, voles and shrews, especially when combined with a wildlife field margin. They in turn attract foxes, badgers, stoats and weasels as well as owls and other birds of prey. Our hedges also provide non-sustaining shelter and insect life for about half of the bat species in Britain as they travel between woodland, feeding area and roosting sites. They include the rare Greater and Lesser Horseshoe Bats which, on warm nights, feed over pastures on beetles, "Daddy-longlegs" (crane flies), moths &c, taking their prey back to a bush or tree on the hedge to eat it.

3.4 Habitats

The two sides of hedge are usually very different, depending on aspect: one being sunny and tending to be drier, and the other shaded and tending to be damper. The vegetation on the hedge has an 'interior' and an 'edge' which varies with its width and composition.

These are modified by the extent and nature of the hedgerow trees. A field margin, ditch, stream or pool often interrelates at the hedge base;

the combination of the two habitats is of greater ecological value than each by itself. Special to Cornish hedges are the combined effects of climate, stone, height and wind-driven salt-burn. Salt-burn extends inland from each coast as far as hill tops in the middle and east of Cornwall. Salt is the active agent which causes the lop-sided wind-blown appearance and reduced height of exposed trees, and provokes the hedgerow inclusion of maritime plants e.g. Alexanders.

An individual hedge often contains a wide range of habitats especially where linking the top of an exposed hill with a sheltered valley bottom.

With the two faces, there are three main wildlife zones: hedge bottom, side and top:-

The hedge bottom is the dampest and most fertile area. It usually reflects the herbage which would naturally grow in the land alongside the hedge and is always richer with an off-set fence, or when a wildlife field margin is left.

The sides of the hedge are the most variable. The nature of wildlife depends on the physical structure of the hedge, its aspect, age and its management. Typically the soil is less fertile than in the fields nearby.

The top of stone hedges may be tending to a dry scree habitat but tops of some Cornish and turf hedges provide a moisture-retentive support for plants that would occur naturally in marsh, scrub or woodland e.g. Royal Fern, Early-Purple Orchid.

All three zones are well-enriched by appropriately managed hedgerow trees providing a variable and dappled shade.

3.5 Wildlife and Trimming

The importance of correct trimming is recognised in the Cornwall County Council's Environmental Charter which seeks to ensure: "The cutting of hedgerows and verges in a manner which helps to maintain flora and fauna, and the encouragement of others to follow the County Council's guidance." This policy can be the more fully implemented with the advice given in this book.

The season and frequency of trimming hedges has a profound effect on wildlife. Trimming with tractor-mounted flails (Chapter 6) started in the 1970s-80s and tended to be an annual summer operation, with a desire to obtain a close cut with a tidy appearance. The use of flail mowers has been frightening in its magnitude, and may be more serious in its total effect than the loss of removed hedges (Bere, 1982). The species-diversity in Cornish hedges is catastrophically reduced when trimming is done each year in the summer months of May to September. The unique sample case study by Carter during 1960-1994 near her home in West Cornwall is helpful. Her hedges are typical of many Cornish hedges and had probably changed little during the preceding 50 years (Margetts & David, 1981). In 1971 she found 188 species of flowering plants in the hedges bordering the randomly selected one mile of country road, hence 2 miles of hedge face (Appendix A gives revised statistics to date). Flailing began in July 1972, continuing thus annually until 1974, then twice each year in May/June and July/August until 1989.

Carter's annual observations showed that by 1985 only 57 species were flowering (Fig.3). The 3 Scarce and 1 Rare species (Red Data Book, 1983) were among the lost. The early vulnerability of annuals and biennials, the monocarpous species, to the summer trimming is clearly shown in figure 4.

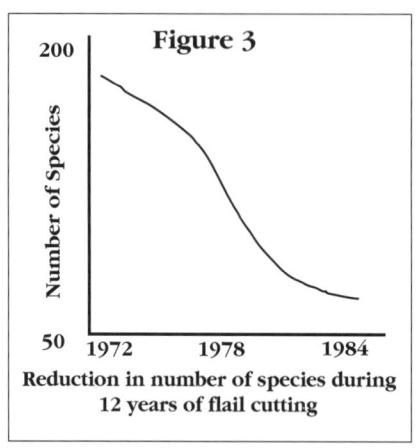

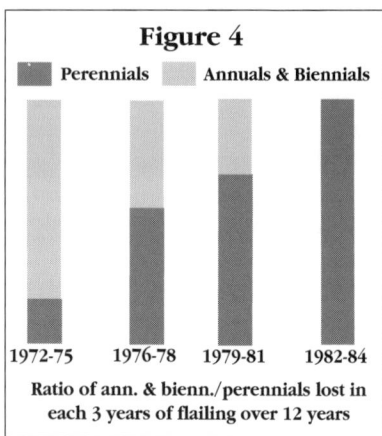

Figure 3
Reduction in number of species during 12 years of flail cutting

Figure 4
Ratio of ann. & bienn./perennials lost in each 3 years of flailing over 12 years

These data correspond with those of Murphy (1985) in her unpublished report on a similar mile of road near Camborne in the period 1971-1985 when she found that 163 plant species were reduced to 117 during a period of mechanical hedge trimming, usually of the less devastating finger-bar type.

Carter has continued her study of the same 2 miles of roadside hedge described above. Flailing was later and only once annually during 1990-92, in October, late July and October. In 1993 she found that of the 94 plant species remaining in 1985, four more had been lost and two reduced in population presumably in the period 1985-89. But 22 of the lost species had reappeared since 1989, 103 species were now flowering again including 27 species blind (not flowering) from 1975-1989, and 27 species had improved in population, eight notably. These data are shown in Appendix A and illustrate the well-known ability of many plant species to rebound when habitat conditions improve. The butterfly count in 1993 showed a similar rebound, with a return of 14 lost species of the original 24 recorded, but with an apparent and understandable time lag in regaining population numbers.

Although a full return to the earlier 188 plant species in Carter's two miles of hedge is problematical, this early improvement demonstrates the effectiveness of a change in the timing of use of the flail. Her data indicate that in general terms the relict population revives immediately flailing times are improved, but that recolonisation takes much longer. She envisages a delay in germination of other annual and biennial plants because the surface of hedges is not normally dug up or scarified. Seed dormancy is often broken by an increase in daylight, either by seasonal demise of shading vegetation, or by the breaking of the soil surface. Neither of these conditions are typically provided by the summer flailing which encourages a tight closely-knit mat of the tougher perennial vegetation, e.g. Ivy. Much of this vegetation is formed of a perpetual carpet of immature plants with an absence of bare patches of soil normally found in traditionally managed hedges. Less-close flailing in winter encourages a multi-storied cover of plants which varies with the season and year, thus providing improved opportunities for species revival.

Some species may be able to recolonise from another habitat; though Carter also looked at the plants (Appendix C) in some of the fields adjoining her roadside hedges, and found that only 37% of the hedgerow species also existed in the fields away from the hedge. Of those, about half were as vulnerable to repeated cropping in the fields as to summer flailing in the hedge.

In Carter's survey, regrettably two-thirds of the hedge food plant species fell victim to the too-tight summer flailing, directly reducing the butterflies found there. The 24 butterfly species seen in 1971 declined to only three in 1985 (Appendix B). This reduction in butterflies recorded by Carter is attributed solely to the summer disturbance by flailing; her observations of these same hedges during the pre-flail years of 1960-71 shewed only the normal seasonal fluctuations. The pre-flail moth population seen by her was also greatly reduced within two years of the introduction of summer flailing. Of the 68 species of moth recorded (as caterpillars or adult) at her hedge in 1971, five relied on plant species absent from the hedge. In 1986, she observed only 19 moth species, including the same five non-hedge feeding species. Species reliant on hedge plants had fallen from 36 to three, while those able to find their foodplant elsewhere, e.g. grass-feeders, fell from 27 to 11. With flailing switched away from summer by 1993, a few of the hedge feeding species returned, including Small Elephant Hawkmoth on Rosebay Willowherb and Mullein Moth on Water Figwort.

Our hedgerow trees are gradually eliminated by frequent close trimming, as evidenced in most parts of Cornwall. Usually they have been felled as a clean-up operation to facilitate trimming, which then prevents regrowth. Not generally realised is that this "short top and sides" maintenance eliminates the characteristic dappled shade required by many plant and animal species. As the diversity of invertebrates and higher animals largely depends on the number of plant species, annual summer close trimming eliminates whole sectors of the wildlife which would otherwise be abundant in Cornish hedges.

Carter observed, during her survey, that because of the tight summer flailing all life including birds, mammals, reptiles and invertebrates, declined in parallel with the loss of plant species, many disappeared within the first few years of the changeover from traditional methods.

Close summer trimming militates against most insect species, and is typified by the absence of our snakes and lizards in those hedges. As the author remembers as a small boy, half a century ago, trying to catch them, they were frequent on the many roadside hedges which were traditionally hand trimmed every winter to about 300mm (12") by the parish roadman. The Common Lizard in Carter's survey was last seen in 1976. The species then remained absent until, after three years of the improved flailing programme, two were seen in the survey hedge at the end of April 1994.

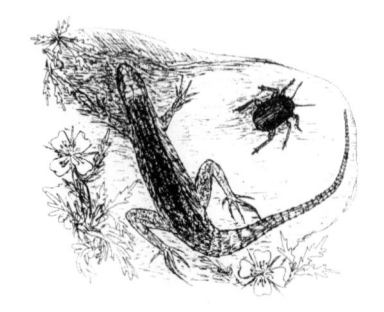

Lizard, Leaf Beetle & Tormentill.

4.

TRADITIONAL HEDGE STRUCTURES IN CORNWALL

Worgan (1811) explained that "All mounds, not regular masonry, are in Cornwall termed hedges". This terminology probably originated in the meaning of the Anglo-Saxon *hecg* referring to a territorial boundary not to be confused with *haeg* a hurdle, or *hega* a living boundary (Dowdeswell 1987); the meaning is similar to 'hedging one's bets'.

Cornish hedges are usually built stone-faced with a subsoil core. Where stone is excessively available, stone hedges are built in similar manner to dry-stone walls in other parts of Britain. Conversely where no stone is present, turf hedges are constructed. Cornish hedges have sloping sides as opposed to walls which have vertical sides, an important distinction not often realised by strangers to Cornwall.

The constructional details of Cornish hedges are extensive and complicated, thus a classification of 21 types of Cornish hedge has been devised (Johnson & Rose, 1994). Because of this wide variation it is useful to make a simple distinction between the average Cornish hedge and its two extremes, the turf hedge and the stone hedge.

In general usage and in this booklet, the broad term Cornish hedge embraces these three main types as described below. There are some unavoidable exceptions where in context the alternative meaning (cf. stone or turf hedge) is understood.

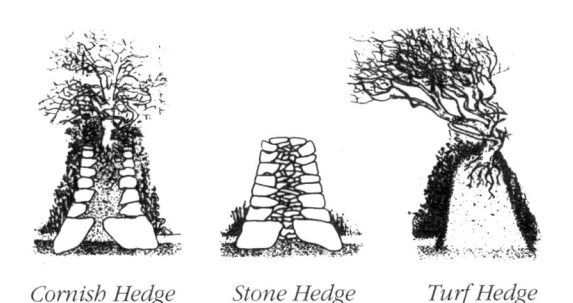

Cornish Hedge   *Stone Hedge*   *Turf Hedge*

4.1 Typical Cornish Hedge

The average Cornish hedge is best described as being a hybrid between a stone wall and an earth bank. It is built of two outer near-vertical layers of local stone with a subsoil core, and is found in most parts of Cornwall, varying in style with the locality and skill of the hedger.

As wide at the base as in height and with tapering sides curved like a Cornish shovel handle or a barrel stave, Cornish hedges range in height from 1m to 3m (3ft - 10ft).

The outer layers of stone are graded in size with the largest stones set as 'grounders' into the top of the subsoil, making a foundation for the hedge. With their size diminishing in the subsequent courses, the stones may be laid flat, upright, or cross-diagonally in herring-bone, according to the locality, and heavily influenced by the type of stone available and the hedger's whim. At intervals of about 400mm (16") up the hedge, a thin layer of turf, about 20mm (0.8") thick, should always be inserted horizontally between the stones. The turf is dug from the hedge base, and traditionally includes 'Stroil' (Couch-grass) which makes for faster knitting of the stones into the hedge. Each hedge has its own subtleties of style which unfortunately tend to be lost when hedging contractors are not properly instructed, and when stone is imported from another district. The hedge core, which provides stability for the hedge, is only made properly from the clayey soft or gritty shale (sometimes decomposed granite) called *rab* found in pockets throughout Cornwall. Rab was used as a road dressing before tarmacadam and every parish has its *rab-pits*. Its composition assists in the bedding of stone in construction, avoids settlement and successfully resists erosion by rain-water. Rab also provides firm anchorage for those shrubs and young trees whose roots do not penetrate down into the field beyond the hedge. It is used up to the top course of stone. Then a dome of top-soil surmounted by turf completes the hedge.

The stability of each stone in a Cornish hedge relies on its shape, its lie and on maintenance of the rab packing material between it and the stones around it. This packing material is held in place and partly converted into humus by the rooting plants growing between the stones. Without this mat of surface roots, the packing material is gradually washed away by rain, eventually causing stones to become loose, fall out and to start a gap in the hedge. Keeping this mat of surface roots relies on good trimming practice, especially avoiding disturbance of summer growth which replenishes the rooting system and protects the hedge from dehydration.

4.2 Turf Hedge

Sometimes known in East Cornwall as a Devon bank, this is an earth core within two outer near-vertical skins, built up in layers, of turf. Its height varies from 1 to 2 metres. Its construction was described by

Charles Vancouver in about 1800 as "raised on a base 7ft wide with a 3ft ditch on each side. The mound was raised 6ft high from its base. The sides faced with turf and left nearly 5ft wide on the top. Planted 2 rows of oak, beech, alder, hazel and hawthorn." (Pollard et al., 1974). Torr (1921) wrote that the removal of Devon banks added ten per cent to farm acreages; but he adds that the gain is offset by the loss of shelter.

Usually the shorter turf hedges are topped with Hawthorn, Blackthorn, Beech or other woody growth being similar in appearance and management to the ordinary thorn hedge set on a low bank, and the ecology will be similarly based. Conversely the taller turf hedges have a distinct side, ecologically separate from the top, which requires protection and trimming similar in most respects to that desirable for the Cornish hedge. The integrity of turf hedges is aided by the periodic winter casting-up of soil from the base. A good side-cover of Hawthorn and Blackthorn, Bramble and Wild Rose is invaluable in preventing livestock from rubbing away the turf. Greater care is needed with a turf hedge than with a Cornish hedge because of its vulnerability to cattle and sheep.

4.3 Stone Hedge

Similar to dry stone walls elsewhere, a stone hedge is usually built with a loose stone core tightly packed between two outer near-vertical layers of coursed stone, including slate and hard shales. Although usually shaped like a Cornish hedge, sometimes it has vertically parallel sides and is called a stone wall. It is often a depository for stones that have been cleared from the fields, and may be as large as 3m (9') in height and/or width. Humus is originally absent and the habitat is stable, with for example stonecrop, lichens, mosses, and Wild Thyme. A notable exception is where climbing plants e.g. Ivy, Honeysuckle have been allowed to climb up the hedge and establish themselves through further rooting in the structure of the hedge itself. Traditionally these climbing plants are pulled out because their expanding rooting habit eventually brings down the hedge. Maintenance of the wildlife need extend no further than the traditional upkeep of the structure of the hedge.

The single stone hedge, usually post-Mediaeval, is less common. It is built up just the width of a stone and colonisation is mainly by lichens; but the gaps between the stones provide opportunity for climbing plants and harbourage for tiny animals. Farmers often allow a half-metre (20") width of Bramble intertwining into a single stone hedge to deter cattle from rubbing themselves on the top stones and bringing them down; this preventative maintenance is encouraged. Seedling trees must be removed before they push the hedge over.

For the visitor, stone hedges are worthy of examination because of the lack of covering vegetation. The styles used in building stone hedges illustrate well the capabilities of the stone and the skills of the hedger. In the slate districts in North Cornwall, the width and thickness of the stone influences the choice of a herring-bone (Jack-and-Jill) style or whether the stone be laid horizontally or vertically. Where granite occurs, the stone is squarer because granite tends to have its grain running both ways at right-angles, so it splits easily into squarish blocks. Conversly the 'elvan' stone, a metamorphosed (cooked) rock, has no easy grain so the hedger is challenged by a variety of shapes which are very difficult to lay successfully in courses. In mid-Cornwall the shale is easily quarried into stones with parallel sides.

While looking at the constructional aspects of stone hedges, one should also note the wildlife which is different and less flamboyant than that in the Cornish hedge.

Stone Hedge

5.

EFFECTS OF RECENT FARMING CHANGES ON TRADITIONAL CORNISH HEDGES.

Traditionally, and within living memory, many Cornish farms were some 8 to 14 hectares (20-35 acres) with a dozen or so Devon or Guernsey cows, a similar number of other cattle, some sheep, pigs and poultry. Corn was grown when pastures were broken and re-sown, and hay was made. Hedges were diligently hand trimmed usually when grass was ploughed in rotation, and in the preparation for corn harvest. Traditional winter management retained the hedges as stockproof boundaries and as shelter whilst protecting them for many centuries and enhancing their biological diversity.

Farms have lately increased more than five-fold in size and livestock numbers, but with few farm workers. Crop rotations have been mechanised and stock diversity simplified. Hand-work in the fields has almost vanished. Modern implements and methods mean a reduced tolerance of small awkward shaped fields, as farmers have to operate in the economic climate influenced by big farms in other parts of Britain, where each field may be the size of a typical Cornish farm. Farmers who move into Cornwall often feel that hedge care is an unwelcome and unnecessary expense; they do not have inherited knowledge of the function and benefit of Cornish hedges in relation to farming and the countryside. To local farmers, hedging is a necessary cost but enjoyed with satisfaction when time can be found.

As the Chairman of the Countryside Commission stated "Gone are the days when farmers could afford to turn to hedging through the winter months. Now payment for this visual amenity helps to boost the rural economy." (Johnson, 1993). The two-pronged attack by government agencies of financial incentives for retention and maintenance, and against removal, is having a considerable influence in those parts of Cornwall where they operate; though unfortunately maintenance and restoration of hedges are often erroneously defined as separate and unrelated functions. This causes much administrative confusion in both central and local government.

The structure of many hedges quickly deteriorates unless the growth is properly managed. When a man with a bill-hook is superceded by a hedge-cutting machine, the hedge ecology is disrupted (Coleman-Cooke, 1965). This was acknowledged by Lord Strathclyde, Under-Secretary of State for the Environment who wrote on 20th July 1992: "The HIS [Hedge

Incentive Scheme] is a carefully targeted scheme aimed at rescuing particular hedgerows of considerable historical and/or wildlife importance which are no longer economically viable. These hedgerows ceased to be managed, thereby becoming overgrown and neglected to the extent that their environmental value has seriously declined."

The abandonment of traditional practices, such as the casting-up, with a Cornish shovel, of soil from ditches along the base of turf hedges on to the hedge top, means that a significant element of the landscape is now at risk.

Controlled rotational grazing of hedges by farm livestock has a beneficial effect on plants by reducing the smothering effects of more vigorous species, but too-tight grazing causes a reduction in species, partly because the hedge becomes drier. For this reason, over-grazing contributes to collapse of some hedge structures.

However, collapse is preferable to the removal of stones and soil; the hedge gradually changes from an agricultural asset to an archaeological feature, and remains as an element of the historic landscape (Countryside Commission, 1994).

The reclamation of rough land and the tidying up of odd corners on farms has meant that many nucleus populations of wildlife are no longer available for the recolonisation of hedges where conditions are at the extreme of the range of particular species. This means that any population crash is likely to result in a local loss of that species.

With the expansion of leisure activities, there is damage to plants just from the increased human pressure (Margetts & David, 1981). Most hedges on farms are valuable in their being protected from public access.

5.1 Effects on Hedge Removal

Removal of hedges accelerated in the post-war years with the use of tractor-drawn trailed implements which required wide headlands. Many hedges were grubbed-out to save the cost of maintenance, a 1.5 hectare (3 acre) field being a good size locally for set-stock grazing the larger dairy herd, or a 4 ha (10 acres) for growing arable crops. With the coming of the swing-shovel, able to lift and sort the stone and even to bury unwanted material, farmers started to remove hedges as often as funds, including government grants, permitted. The economics of larger fields continue to attract hedge removal, and there is an added incentive where town planners encourage weathered stone for facing to new or converted buildings. Hedge removal is not new, but today it is much easier and the apparent rewards much greater.

The extent of hedge removal anywhere in Cornwall varies with the background and personality of each farmer. For example, a Sussex farmer who moved into West Cornwall removed most of the hedges and reorganised his dairy farm in large fields with barbed wire fences as field boundaries. Neighbouring farmers, with a closer understanding of the local environment, have not removed any hedges within living memory. Where income from the land is of less importance, as on many part-time farms, there is often a deep reluctance to alter the landscape by hedge removal. Nevertheless there are enough farmers intent on enlarging their fields for there to be an estimated current loss of 2% each year (T.Edwards, pers. comm.).

5.2 Effects on Maintenance Needs of Hedges

"If properly managed, hedges may be termed impregnable to the attempts at least of cattle" (Worgan, 1811). Hedge maintenance involves the interrelated jobs of trimming of the vegetation and repair of the structure. Hedge repair is a complex subject outside the scope of this book.

Today the routine repair of Cornish hedges is seldom economical where livestock, other than the docile local breeds, are pastured, unless the hedge is protected by barbed wire or electric fence. Changed economics have brought in continental cattle and hill sheep breeds and their crosses, with their inbred propensity to roam. On Bodmin Moor the introduction of nimble-footed sheep, able to climb over the old boundaries, encourages the use of wire fencing (Countryside Commission, 1994). Larger livestock farms hold a greater concentration of cattle or sheep within a field, increasing the urge to break out and thus exerting more than traditional pressure on the hedges. Hedges with a weak structure cannot restrain these larger herds and flocks of non-traditional breeds without the addition of wire.

Rubbing-posts, granite pillars 2-2.5m (6-8ft) in length set about 0.6m (2ft) in the ground, many being prehistoric men-hirs, are still found in some fields. Cattle rub on them instead of on the hedges. Mr S. Parry (pers. comm. 1993) remembers moving granite rubbing-posts from grass-field to grass-field some 60 years ago, as the plough went round Nanpusker Farm at Hayle. Their re-introduction, or the positioning of large rocks in lieu, is desirable to lessen damage to hedges. Some farmers have reduced nitrogen dressings in order to encourage clover and other non-grass species; this reversion to permanent pasture tends to reduce the desire of livestock to break out.

On non-livestock farms, direct damage to hedges is limited to impact by machinery and by weather; but where damage does inevitably occur, there is little incentive to effect repairs because of the absence of livestock. Close ploughing reduces support for grounders and causes collapse. The value of hedges for crop shelter is probably underestimated. Establishing a wildlife field margin reduces the need for maintenance.

The effect of fallowing land (set-aside) is to reduce the need for hedge trimming while the field is uncropped. By not trimming, the habitats are improved but care must be taken not to allow the growth to become too mature for the hedge-cutting machinery.

Modern farming, with fewer working on the land, means that hedges are less often repaired at the first sign of damage. Before they are repaired, weaknesses in the stonework become gaps in the hedge and there is a tendency for some farmersto attempt crude repairs using a tractor fore-end-loader. These seldom knit together fully and they tend to perpetuate the hedge weakness. Most of this work can be avoided by a combination of correct trimming and fencing.

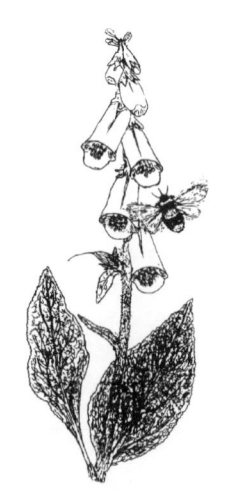

Bumble-bee and foxglove

6.

METHODS OF TRIMMING CORNISH HEDGES.

Traditional trimming with hook and slasher (a heavy hook on a long handle) kept the workers in autumn and winter and left a natural length of 300mm (12") of vegetation on the hedge sides. Today this hand work is uneconomic and mechanised trimming is a great boon to farmers. It gives easily a tidy and organised urban-like appearance to the farm at a reasonable cost. Unfortunately the habit has arisen of trimming too often and too tight on sides and top; this is needlessly expensive for farmers and results in eventual destruction of most of the hedgerow trees in the landscape. Thus the shelter and nutritional values of hedges for crops and stock in coastal and upland areas are being progressively reduced year after year.

Many hedges still retain weakened survivors of Thorns, Elm, Ash and Sycamore which quickly become bushes and trees again if allowed. Unfortunately a lot have vanished from other hedges which have been tight-trimmed for a long time.

Tight machine-trimming predisposes hedges to dry out in the summer; some do not recover full moisture for several years. This desiccation causes a serious reduction in plant species, and deterioration of the hedge structure by consequent erosion of inter-stone packing material. Bare hedges give a faster run-off of rain with more erosion. A dried hedge-core coupled with heavy rain often results in stones falling away from the hedge-face. Dessicated hedges suffer population crashes in susceptible plants and animals, and loss of the species if summer flailing continues.

Most farmers, because of their cropping rotation and hedge structures, have to trim their hedges regularly with a flail. The modern farm flail is a hydraulically-driven cutting-head mounted on a swinging arm attached to a tractor, and comprises a number of heavy blades pivoted along a shaft which is driven at about 500 rpm (Fig. 5).

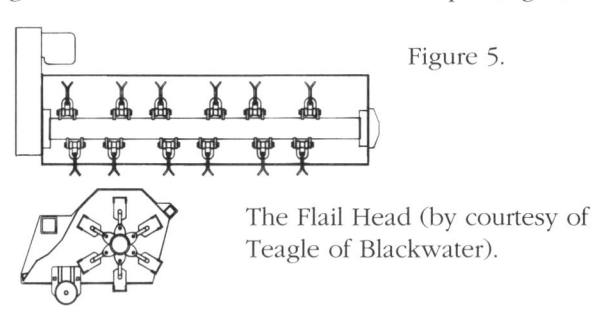

Figure 5.

The Flail Head (by courtesy of Teagle of Blackwater).

This example is made locally by Teagle at Blackwater and cuts a 1.3m (4'3") swath, trimming branches of 40mm (1½") Blackthorn to 60mm (2½") Sycamore in diameter which represents about 4 years of growth, varying in locality. There is no mechanical justification for an annual trim.

The flail is a brutal machine which has a tearing, not a cutting, action. It causes excessive sap bleeding and its cyclone hammering plays havoc with much of the invertebrate population. The dense mulch resulting from flailing leafed hedges in summer has a bad smothering effect on delicate plants, and encourages the harmful spread of rampant species. Flailing less often and in winter, and omitting any horizontal cut across the top of the hedge, reduces mulching damage and species mortality. Even winter trimming destroys many hibernating insects and the potential egg-laying sites for those insects which select the previous year's new growth for this purpose (Fry & Lonsdale, 1991). So hedges should be trimmed at these intervals of not less than 3-5 years or so, and in rotation around the farm instead of doing all the hedges in one year.

In careful hands the flail is a machine which although much to be regretted is capable, with the aid of protective wire, coppicing, and well-timed trimming, of restoring hedges in Cornwall to most of their former glory.

Teagle, in the instructions for using their flail, advise: "When using the machine, particularly for the first time on a hedge, try to cut along a straight line rather than follow the 'ins and outs' of the present contour. Do not try to cut hedges too close. Try to induce the growth of a thick face on the hedge." Instead of trying to trim the sides to a uniformly close cut of 100mm-200mm (4"-8"), the tractor-drivers should be content with a variable cut of 250mm-450mm (12"-18") which results from driving faster beside the irregular hedge. This saves money whilst increasing the range of hedge habitat. They should feel that they are skimming off the excess growth instead of giving a tight and tidy "short top & sides". This is totally different from the management of ordinary Hawthorn hedges elsewhere as summarised in Berryman (1993). Trimming around telegraph and other poles in the hedge is cheaper when done without slowing down; the resulting untidy scrub growth around each pole is useful to wildlife and it tones down the effect of a naked pole in the landscape.

Traditionally the top of the Cornish hedge was allowed to grow up and be controlled by coppicing. Using modern equipment today, the top of the hedge should be trimmed each side at an angle of roughly 60° so as to leave about 0.5m to 1m (2'-3') width untrimmed along the top of the hedge. This technique ensures that the tree growth emerges along the centre line of the hedge, making subsequent management of the hedge easier. Shrubby and tree growths including Elm suckers then develop naturally out of the hedge top. A woodland-margin hedge is one of the few situations where a horizontal cut across the top is justified.

Exposed wind-blown field hedges should receive the vertical pass on both sides followed by a higher and sloping cut on the down-wind side, leaving the centre of the hedge to battle upwards against the salt-laden wind.

Many farmers, less interested in profit, allow their hedges to grow out into the field. Livestock enjoy the shelter of Hawthorn, Blackthorn, Bramble, Elm and Sycamore; further invasion is controlled by the yearly pasture topping in autumn. Because less light and rain get to the actual hedge side, it may break down when assaulted by livestock and need protection by wire. In these situations barbed wire or netting is difficult to erect properly. Even so, it can usually be adequately secured, and the landscape and wildlife values of this style of hedge management are great.

Some very traditional farmers keep the old custom of trimming their hedge sides only when the pastureland is ploughed in rotation and when corn is harvested. This admirable practice, ideal for conservation, relies on good hedge structure, slow growth and usually protective wire.

A few farmers routinely spray their Cornish hedge-sides instead of trimming; for example a systemic herbicide used around the farm to destroy all plant growth behind a mains electric fence. This is bad practice because, apart from the overall ecological damage, spraying tends to kill out the plant species which maintain the inter-stone packing material of the hedge. Eventually stones will fall out and the hedge structure start to collapse. Where a previously-fertilised hedge is infested by aggressive plant species (e.g. Nettle, Cleavers) there is no advantage in spraying these to hasten natural regeneration, because nature itself will do the job better as the high fertility diminishes.

Exceptionally difficult invasive plants, e.g. Japanese Knotweed, may be spot-sprayed by knapsack, provided a correct narrow-spectrum chemical is used and applied while the foliage is young. Repeated hard flailing to ground level is more successful, starting with the new growth in spring. Annual treatment of survivors is necessary, whether sprayed or cut.

6.1 Hedges not on farms.

The traditional use every winter of a hook aided by a crooked stick is a simple and cheap way of looking after a Cornish hedge in villages and towns.

Getting the right tools and using them correctly is the secret of trimming Cornish hedges in the traditional way. Using a hook is well worth learning properly, and is a skill that once acquired is never lost.

With a little practice, using a hook is quick, and when used correctly in winter, leaves a consistent length of 300mm (12") of growth. The domestic strimmer is slower, expensive, more hazardous and, especially in summer months, cuts much too tightly.

By waiting until well after the first frosts, most of the summer growth has died back and the animals have gone into their winter quarters. Trimming is then kinder to wildlife and very much easier. Using the hook properly gives a tidy finish of about 300mm (12").

In sheltered localities, flowering Greater Stitchwort, in which the Piskys are reputed to hide during daytime (Davey, 1909), and Red Campion are useful indicators of good management.

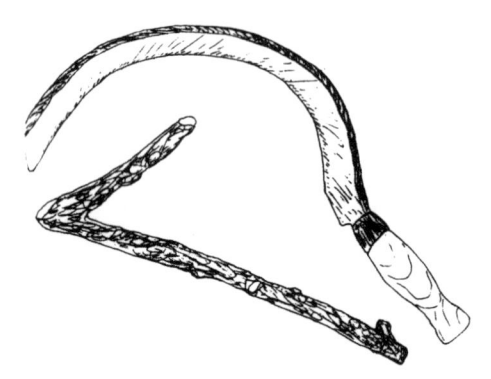

Hook and Stick - traditional tools

6.1.1 Equipment:

Second-hand hooks may be purchased for £1-£2. A new, quality hook costs £12-£15 and should be bought from a farmers' supplier. The hook may seem heavy but is just the right weight for trimming hedges, and lasts a lifetime. Beware of any hook which has an off-set handle; this is not the best one for using on a hedge. Lighter hooks, which are designed for cutting long grass, do not have the weight to cut through the annual growth of Blackthorn, and their blades tend to break.

Tall or woody hedges may need a heavy slasher, costing new about £30. This is about 1.4m (4½ ft) long and has a strong blade set on a stout handle. It will easily cut coppice growth 50mm (2") in diameter, and again is a lifetime's investment.

The secret of easy trimming is to keep the hook sharp. A sharpening 'scythe stone' is needed, and can be bought from the local farmers' suppliers. Modern bench grinders or disc cutters will suffice, but cannot be taken to the job, and result in many trips to-and-fro, or a useless blunt hook.

A crook makes the job much easier and more effective. The crooked stick cannot be purchased; it is cut from the hedge and lasts many seasons. It has the shape of a tick ✓, and should be about 400-600mm (16"-24") long, depending on the reach of the worker, with a short side branch about 150mm (6") coming out at an angle of 60° - 80°. If the angle is more acute, the crook will get entangled, if near a right-angle of 90° it will not gather the growth properly. A crook from Blackthorn, Hazel, Ash or Elm is very suitable and like all timber, is more pleasant to handle after being allowed to season by drying out naturally.

Finally, gloves are advisable for the householder.

6.1.2 Method:

First, choose fine dry days from November-March for the work. Typically the side of the hedge will have a year's tangled growth of brambles, together with some seedling trees, Blackthorn suckers and the remains of the season's plant growth.

Traditional trimming is easy and fast when the right method is used. It starts at the highest point that is easily reached and works downwards, in contrast to the up-stroke trimming of English thorn hedges.

The hook is held in the preferred hand, and is used in downward cutting strokes. The knuckles of this hand will be as close to the hedge as possible and the cutting strokes of the hook are made parallel to the hedge side. Novices often make the error of keeping their hand too far from the hedge with the result that the cutting action is not parallel with the hedge side; this makes the job much harder and gives an untidy finish.

The crook is held in the other hand by the end of the long handle, with the crook facing downwards. The action of the crook is at right-angles to the hedge and roughly parallel with the ground. It has two functions: helping the actual cut, and then getting the severed vegetation on to the ground clear of the hedge.

Firstly the end of the crook is inserted into the growth located at the top of the intended cutting stroke of the hook. Then the crook with the attached growth is pulled away from the hedge with the result that the growth tautens so that the hook can cut it without sliding down the growth ineffectively.

The hook cuts the growth, which is held by the crook, between the crook and the hedge one or more times until it is severed from the hedge.

Next the crook is inserted into the growth immediately below the vegetation which has just been cut, and the process repeated. This is done several times until the bottom is reached. Thus a vertical swath has been cut.

When done properly, the cut growth will have been peeled off by the crook like the skin off an orange. Using several more pulls at the growth, the crook neatly makes a small pile of the severed vegetation just outside the feet of the worker. As he works along the hedge cutting swath after swath, he is able to walk in the space between the cut growth and the hedge itself.

A blunt hook makes for hard work and does an untidy job. Where the growth is tough, almost as much time should be spent in sharpening the hook as in using it!

Finally the cut vegetation ('browse') is gathered up with a long-handled fork ('eavil') and deposited in a spare corner to provide a temporary habitat. The stems of the browse will house many tiny over-wintering insects which are killed if it is burnt (Fry & Lonsdale, 1991).

Before putting the tools away, it is customary to give the hook and/or slasher a good sharpen, and a wipe with an oily rag so as to be ready for the next time.

Campion and Greater Stitchwort

7.

CLOSE AND OFF-SET WIRE FENCES.

In today's harsh economic climate, fencing-wire is an important factor in the preservation of the wildlife and structure of most Cornish hedges.

Traditionally, and today within the older generation, for a farmer to use barbed wire was seen as a public admission of sloppy farming. Many livestock farmers still are proud that they have no barbed wire fences but do agree that their policy is uneconomic. On some of these farms without barbed wire in West Cornwall it has been estimated that, typically, a length equivalent to the total of field hedges on the farm is rebuilt about once every 100-150 years. This is an overall figure, some lengths would have been rebuilt several times, others not at all.

"With close wire protection, the repair of weak hedges is usually reduced by nine-tenths."

The decision to wire hedges depends on the farmer's livestock, his crop policy and on the extent and vigour of Thorn, Bramble and Rose species on the hedge side. At the one extreme, a weak turf hedge cannot function properly without a fence; but at the other, a well-built high stone hedge requires no protection. Emphasis is placed on the need for wire to be put up and kept taut, otherwise livestock find their way out. Plain wire may be used for horses.

7.1 Close Wiring

For the best results for farm livestock and wildlife, barbed wire and/or netting should be set tight against the actual structure of the hedge. This is after the growth on the side of the hedge has been trimmed as tightly as possible with the flail. The fencing posts are driven into the ground as close to the hedge bottom as its foundation stones allow, and the wire stapled to the posts. Afterwards the hedge is trimmed in the normal way outside the wire, with a variable thickness of growth remaining behind the wire owing to the irregular hedge structure. This encourages a wide range of plants. It discourages stock from damaging the stone or turf face of the hedge, while allowing useful non-grass grazing. The hazard of wire entanglement for the flail ensures that a good cover of vegetation is kept. The wire lasts 10-30 years depending on sea exposure; dipping the wire in wet bitumen is messy but effective in prolonging its life in our salty atmosphere. In localities where hedge growth is vigorous, how soon the posts will rot is immaterial because after several years the wire becomes firmly embedded within the vegetation. If the hedge growth is weak, eventually the remains of the wire can be pulled out, the side of the hedge trimmed back hard, new wire erected and the process repeated.

For pure-bred lowland sheep without lambs, two strands of barbed wire carefully erected are sometimes enough. Hill breeds of sheep and their crosses are less traditional to Cornwall and without proper pig-netting they will push in anywhere and eventually destroy the hedge. Netting should be set close to the hedge structure so as to avoid sheep being trapped behind it, but far enough away to prevent climbing up the hedge side. The netting must be strained tight to accept sheep browsing through it during early years.

Alternatively where the structure of the hedge (or a ha-ha wall) allows, a single strand, or for sheep two strands, may be attached to posts stuck horizontally into the side of the hedge or wall, at about 1m (3') above the ground. This traditional practice has lapsed in recent years but works well when the posts are carefully selected and able to be inserted into the hedge without damaging the structure. The wire does not have to be very tight, so lessening the need for intermediate straining posts. Although cheaper to erect, it needs more care. Barbed wire is suitable for sheep but is of less value for cattle which may rub on the posts either breaking them or loosening stones in the hedge. Mains-fencing electrified wire can be used for cattle or sheep. Livestock graze the hedge below the wire, thus fully utilising the field.

Many farmers put an ordinary fence on the top of their weak hedges to stop the animals from climbing over. This is bad practice because the damage by farm animals to the hedge-side does not have to be repaired to keep them in. Eventually the whole hedge is run down out into the field and the cattle escape under the fence! Top wiring is acceptable only where there is a low hedge of structure good enough to withstand stock climbing up it year after year.

An old sheet of corrugated iron is sometimes invaluable as a temporary shield where stock have rubbed or burrowed, provided it is set out 500 mm (18") to allow growth to re-establish and removed before it smothers the new plants. Alternatively, applied cattle dung or slurry is an effective temporary deterrent.

7.2 Off-set Wiring

Many farmers, particularly those in East Cornwall with low or weak turf hedges, use off-set permanent fences erected about 1m (1yd) from the hedge base, the hedge being trimmed behind the wire. The off-set fence requires one or two strands of barbed wire, or high tensile mains-electrified wire, which is tightly strained with straining posts at each change in direction: expensive with meandering older hedges. Additional strands or netting may be added to protect the hedge from the ravages of a flock of sheep.

Unfortunately the conservation value of the field strip between these fences and the hedge is reduced by the hedge being trimmed too tight. The 1m (1yd) set-out recommended by the Agricultural Development and Advisory Service (Berryman, 1993) is too narrow because it does not allow for the full development of the hedge. The problem is that there is not enough room to run the flail.

In recent years opinion has changed. The offset fence is now often used with a 2m (2yds) wide wildlife margin to make a very worthwhile fieldside environment, combining hedge and field margin. Unless the fence is set out quite far, at least 1.5m (4'6") or 2m (6') depending on the shape of the hedge, the flail cannot leave enough plant cover on the hedge and tends to knock out stones.

Another method with an arable/grass rotation is to use a temporary off-set fence of barbed or electric wire which is removed when the grass is ploughed up. A battery operated one/two-reel electric fencing system is easily moved around the farm with the animals. Shifting the fence eliminates the need to control growth beneath it. The hedge habitat is looked after because trimming can be done in the winter and, in the absence of the fence, there is less tendency to trim too tight.

Shorting-out of permanent electric fences by plant growth from the ground beneath may be prevented expensively by using a strimmer or preferably a scythe. Where herbicide spray is used, it should be applied under the wire in as narrow a strip as possible . Sometimes the height of the bottom live wire can be set so that livestock graze under it. Neutral-coloured or wooden posts, black insulators and stranded-steel wire are visually less obnoxious than the conspicuous orange-coloured posts, insulators and wire often used.

7.3 Tenancy Agreements

Many tenancy agreements have clauses which require tenants "to put and keep their hedges in traditional repair"; or, in similar words, "to repair maintain and keep in good and substantial order and condition their live and dead hedges and field-walls". This has, in the past been taken to mean that hedges have to be closely trimmed, sides and top, with no barbed wire set into the hedge. Usually there is no actual prohibition, in the tenancy agreement, of wire in association with the hedge or field-wall. The assumption that barbed wire cannot be used has often been a local interpretation with its origin in the practice of bad tenants of putting barbed wire where the Cornish hedge requires actual repair. But where the hedge is in good structural condition, close-wiring that is embedded in properly trimmed side-growth is of much advantage to an incoming tenant. Off-set wiring may be equally acceptable in appropriate circumstances. Conversely an unsound hedge that has been fenced along its top is likely to attract considerable dilapidation monies, both for repairs to the hedge and for removal and disposal of the fence.

More importantly there is some doubt as to whether a hedge which is traditionally maintained and trimmed without protective wire, but which will not keep in the intensively-grazed modern Friesian cow or the more wayward beef breeds, could be said to be in good tenantable repair and condition.

Hedges should be trimmed and coppiced in rotation over several years; and landlords are entitled to receive them as such at the end of the tenancy unless stated otherwise in the agreement.

Side-growth trimmed as recommended in the Guidance Note is likely to meet normal tenancy requirements. Many hedges in East Cornwall are a low turf hedge with a planted Thorn hedge on top; these have been traditionally cut-and-laid. The management of top-growth on the more substantial turf hedges and Cornish hedges varies considerably. Some estates require periodic cutting-and-laying, others, in the interests of shelter and amenity, expect the tenants not to cut any scrub and trees on the hedge top. In many cases, the agreement clauses relate to rural practices long gone, and may be unenforceable today. To avoid disputes at term end, it is recommended that early action is taken to bring tenancy agreements up to date. To uphold the rental and conservation value of the estate, landlords and tenants should exchange letters agreeing that the live component of the hedges shall be managed in accordance with the Guidance Note at the start of this booklet, which sets out practical measures meeting the interests of both parties.

This opinion relates only to the live component, the plant and tree growths, of a Cornish hedge. Agreement clauses for the maintenance of the dead component, the earth/stone structure, should remain in force unaltered.

The inherent question is one of damage to the reversionary interests of the landlord. A relevant Court decision may be desirable before the issues become clear.

Many tenants may be tempted by an increasing number of conservation grants for hedges promoted by various government departments and agencies. Some of these are designed to develop the wildlife potential of the hedge and may pay scant regard to the husbandry pratices properly expected by a landlord of his tenant. In such instances, the prudent tenant obtains the written approval of his landlord to such work before he embarks on the scheme.

Navelwort

8.

WILDLIFE FIELD MARGINS.

During the post-war period of food shortages farmers were encouraged, with fertiliser grants and guaranteed prices, to maximise food production and to crop every available acre right up to the hedge. Successive governments encouraged hedge removal everywhere in Britain. Nowadays with European over-production, profits can only be made on farms where unit costs of production are low. Although no farmer intends to waste natural or artificial fertiliser or crop sprays on his hedges, realistically the placement of fertilisers and sprays is not entirely accurate. Without a field margin or headland, the hedges often receive costly spray and fertiliser intended for the field. Inept tractor driving results in hedges being enriched excessively.

Farmers know that the 1-2m (1-2yds) wide margin around the outside edge of a small field is a significant proportion of the field, and therefore of the crop. But crops usually yield less in this marginal strip and so, in today's economic conditions, the profitability of cropping field margins is questioned.

Hedgerows and field margins provide habitats with over-wintering densities sometimes exceeding 1000 insects per square metre. A layman may think that this huge quantity threatens the welfare of the fieldcrop, but this is not so because about 10% are predators which move out into the field, reducing pest numbers significantly, while other insect species stay within the diverse habitats of the hedge and field margin. The hedge itself has a nett benefit as a source of the natural enemies of pests, including the ground beetles, ladybirds and parasitic wasps (Fry & Lonsdale, 1991), and attracts the birds which work over the field for pests.

Hitherto many farmers have concentrated on direct control of aphids and other plant feeders by spraying expensively with pesticides, killing the predators incidentally. Research at various Universities and other centres is showing that predators are more mobile than previously thought, and that they multiply to numbers appropriate to the pest numbers, thus restoring the balance of nature. Birds flock in response to availability of prey, and lay larger clutches when pest numbers increase (Carrington, 1898). Many beetle species start out from hedges in early April and, by the end of May, more than one-quarter of them will be in the field over 60m (66yds) away from the hedge. Wood mice with radio-collars have travelled 1 kilometre (0.6 mile) through fields during a single night.

Sarah Carter's roadside hedges.

Sheltered prehistoric lane.

Too neat-and-tidy for good wildlife.

Coppiced trees on hedge.

A stone hedge rebuilt about 200 years ago.

The ruined Wheal Mary engine-house mid-left.

Typical flail mounted on tractor.

Research has indicated that fields of more than 5 hectares (12 acres) should be divided by a wildlife ridge of rough vegetation, equivalent to a 0.4m (16") high Cornish hedge, to give harbourage for predators. Most Cornish fields are smaller, already surrounded by hedges and, where traditionally maintained, are well-served by predators.

Predator number and versatility is considerably improved by the creation of a wildlife margin around the field. Diversity in plants and animals, especially at the foot of the hedge, is greater than it would be in the hedge and field margin if separate. This combined value is most significant when the hedge is looked after traditionally with a scrubby and coppiced tree component. Animals which shelter in the hedge find much of their food in the margin. The increase in the total food supply is of special benefit to those bird species of value to the farmer in their control of weed seeds and insect pests. One important result is that more species become self-sustaining in the hedge and no longer have to rely on another habitat for population replenishment following hard times. But both habitats are totally reliant on sympathetic management; Carter found, not surprisingly, that the same species tended to be lost to annual summer flailing in the hedge and to repeated cropping in the fields; and that these are usually the species whose loss is the more regretted.

8.1 Arable Fields

The wise arable farmer leaves a 1-2m (1-2yds), perhaps 3m strip untilled around his fields. The economic cost of this is more than offset by saving the cost of summer spraying for aphids. The margin also saves money on fertilizer and other sprays as it is left untreated. It gives some protection to the crop from rabbit damage as they browse mainly on the margin close to their burrows.

During field cultivations, the field margin is used as a turning headland. The action of turning machinery, in causing wheel track scuffling and compaction, engineers its own habitat variation. These tiny areas of bare ground are used by a variety of burrowing insects, such as tiger beetle larvae and solitary bees and wasps. By heating up quickly in sunshine, they give a micro-climate advantage to those insects needing to bask (Fry & Lonsdale, 1991).

The wildlife field margin needs proper creation and management. Local wildlife experts are usually happy to give advice. Ideally the strip should start by being clean of volunteer crop plants and noxious perennial weeds. Autumn herbicide spraying and/or rotovation followed by traditional ploughing makes for a good start.

Once established, mowing during the convenient interval between harvest and cultivation for the next crop controls the bramble, scrub and seedling trees, while the flowering plants have been allowed to ripen and cast their seed. Margins do not always require mowing annually but may be left two or more years depending on scrub growth. The statutory weeds e.g. Ragwort and Thistle must have their tops skimmed off before seeding. Subsequently, apart from the autumn toppings, the best and cheapest action is to let Nature to take its course.

Exceptionally, on sites where the natural vegetation including dormant seed has been destroyed, plants and invertebrates appropriate to the locality may be encouraged by digging during winter occasional turves, each about 200mm (8") square, from suitable habitats nearby and laying them at every 3m to 5m (10'-16') along the margin.

The Game Conservancy Council has recommended the sowing of grasses, with either Cocksfoot at 3 gm/m^2, Yorkshire Fog at 4 gm/m^2, or preferably equal proportions of each at 3.5 gm/m^2 (Wratten, 1993). In environmental terms, this is an overly crude way of providing a wildlife field margin hosting a relatively low number of plant species and a limited range of predators. It is not recommended. Fry & Lonsdale (1991) advise the use of a nurse crop such as annual Westerwolds ryegrass; this is unnecessary in the mild Cornish climate and self-seeding could prove difficult to prevent without drastic summer trimming of the site.

Natural regeneration (MAFF, 1993) "will often be the most practical way of establishing a cover. It can also benefit the environment by providing feeding grounds for birds and encouraging a diversity of flora. Natural regeneration following cereals provides winter feeding grounds for seed-eating birds. The flora encourages insects, providing foods for insectivorous birds. Light and shallow soils are especially suitable for natural regeneration since a greater variety of flora will often appear on such land. Farmers may want to give special thought to natural regeneration in areas where birds associated with arable land are in decline". Unfertilized natural regeneration is inexpensive and, in the long term, much more attractive to wildlife than reseeding or tree-planting. Just ....

" Plough it and leave it!"

An old-fashioned high-cut furrow produces the right unevenness of finish for the greatest plant diversity. Purchased wild flower seed mixtures are not needed and should be avoided because of the likelihood of introducing new plant varieties.

Cornish weather gives a long growing season which ensures easier and quicker natural regeneration than in other parts of Britain.

Sarah Carter's species list (Appendix C) for recently ploughed fields next to her surveyed hedges shows the strength of the weed-seed bank in West Cornwall. She found 124 species of flowering plants and 28 grasses in several grass fields which had been sprayed off, cultivated, planted with daffodil bulbs and left untreated for one year. These fields were unusual because this crop allowed for a season's germination of weeds in an uncompetitive situation. Of the flowering plant species, over half had been identified in the adjoining roadside hedge, being just over one-third of the hedgerow species total.

In the fields with a prior history of more cropping than the others, there were heavy concentrations of a few robust plant species, while others were persisting though diminished. These fields showed a depleted seed-bank with fewer species overall and a much higher proportion of noxious varieties and residual crop plants such as clover and rape. Only fields with the least earlier cropping produced a maximum count with almost all of the total species present. About one-fifth of the species were spread widely, but thinly, across all field types.

These data show clearly the immense value of the weed-seed bank in the typical Cornish field, both for providing a wide variety of food plants in the wildlife field margin and, given the opportunity, for replenishing an impoverished hedge. They also confirm that these seeds remain viable for many years in the undisturbed soil. Some 28 of the species found are the primary foodplants for butterflies and the larger moths (Appendix C); a further 42 may be eaten by caterpillars in the absence of their preferred plant.. The distribution between the different fields shows that about half of the butterfly and moth plant species may soon be lost under continuous arable cropping because they are prevented from replacing their germinated seed. This early loss of the more beneficial and interesting species, then replaced by noxious weeds, shows a similar disruption of the cycle of reproduction and distribution to that which occurs in Cornish hedges as the result of summer too-close trimming.

Economically the arable farmer can allow the plants in his field margin opportunity to flower and cast seed before the autumn topping. To keep control he should cultivate the margin perhaps every five to seven years (old saying: "one year's seeding makes seven years' weeding"). This cultivation delays evolution of the field margin to low scrub, replenishes its wild flower seed-bank and gives the opportunity for some control of perennial weeds which do not easily respond to herbicides.

Many arable farmers use a non-cropped 'sterile strip' to separate the wildlife field margin from the field crop. Its function is to act as a barrier for undesirable plants, yet allows predators easy access to the field. Its width varies from 1-2m (1-2yds) depending on the way it is created and maintained:-
1) Rotovated with one pass. This is probably the most cost-effective.
2) Sown with permanent grass, and close-mown at about 100mm (4"). Unless mown frequently, it gradually becomes weed infested and loses its value as a barrier.
3) Sprayed with a total herbicide each year. This eliminates awkward weeds including brome grass and cleavers but is unacceptable to some farmers because it disrupts the wildlife food chain. Spraying may be by contact, systemic or residual herbicide. A spray skirt is needed to protect the field margin and the hedge. Rarely, selected narrow-spectrum herbicides or weed-wipe may be used where adjoining crops are economically threatened by one weed species becoming temporarily rampant.

Recent changes in agricultural policy have resulted in farmers being encouraged or compelled to set aside land to various states of bare or bastard fallow, or to specified non-food crops. The rules for fallowing set-aside land will always be changing and the field margin has to be managed accordingly. This may mean that when the fallow period is for several years, the margin may not need to be annually topped, but may be ploughed with the rest of the field at the end of the years of fallowing.

In 1993 farmers had the choice of setting aside 15% or 18% of their arable land for rotational (<1 year) or non-rotational (>5 years). For land in rotational set-aside, the land must be mown at a height of 10cm (4") between 15th July and 15th August or cultivated by 31st August. Although this requirement has a deleterious effect on the plant population generally (MAFF may give special exemptions), it is before Thistle, Dock and Ragwort set seed, and therefore these weeds are controlled according to the rules of the scheme. For land in non-rotational set-aside, there is no requirement for cutting, unless the field will be used for grazing when a 10cm (4") cut between the same dates is specified.

Farmers who wish to manage their set-aside land in a particularly effective way for wildlife are encouraged to apply to MAFF for exemptions. The author's experience suggests that an application for exemption, which is technically sound, is not refused unless it is actually banned by a MAFF regulation. Wildlife is generally better served by a mowing of 30cm (12") during the second half of August or early the trunk varies with exposure to salt-laden winds, some trees taking 40 or more years to reach this size, others never getting big enough for coppicing, especially above the 600ft contour (Allaby, 1981). It is important to realise that only the trunks of this size are taken, being cut where convenient, usually at about 200-600mm (8"-24") above ground. The other smaller trunks from the same coppiced stool remain to be cut in their turn during later years, thus maintaining continuity of habitat (Fry & Lonsdale, 1991).

This selective coppicing encourages many of the climbing plants (e.g. Honeysuckle, Black Bryony) which, whilst requiring support, are easily smothered by a large tree canopy (Dowdeswell, 1987). There is some evidence that young coppice regrowth is a more succulent food for wildlife than growth on mature trees or seedlings (Fry & Lonsdale, 1991). It provides shelter for hedgerow birds from predators (Pollard et al., 1974) and essential perches for many song birds and birds of prey e.g. Buzzard.

The Agricultural Advisory and Development Service (ADAS) recommends that 5-10% of the hedge length should be coppiced each year on a 10-20 year rotation (Berryman, 1993). In many tightly-trimmed hedges there remain survivors which will become trees when allowed to grow properly. These can then be coppiced in the traditional way.

A felling licence is required when coppicing growths exceeding 150mm (6") in diameter. The authorities are usually sympathetic to hedgerow coppicing operations where the landowner is managing his hedges in a traditional manner, and consults beforehand. Generally a trailer-load of logs once a year does not attract the wrath of the Forestry authority. But some trees may have a Tree Preservation Order which entails getting consent from the local planning authority before starting work.

Coppicing gives a constant supply of firewood "finding the farm-house in fuel" (Worgan, 1811). A nearby householder with a woodburning stove is often available and anxious to carry out, free, the yearly coppicing. The potential renewable annual crop from our hedges in Cornwall may be about 15,000 tonnes, with about 20% available energy. Any cut wood including the twigs, which can be left on top of the hedge to rot away, will be gratefully received by the wildlife.

The shade cast by uncoppiced hedgerow trees has a significant effect on crop production depending on the height of the tree and the length of its side branches. Dowdeswell (1987) states that the effect on crops is found to be appreciable only up to a distance of one or two times the height of the tree-top from the base of the hedge. The coppiced hedge has therefore little shading effect on crops, compared with mature trees which may affect production perhaps some 15m (16yds) out into the field.

The wind permeability of coppiced hedges is near to the optimum of 40%, giving a reduction of around 20% in wind speed at the hedge bottom and some appreciable shelter leewards of about 50m (55yds) (Dowdeswell, 1987). Conversely isolated mature trees create swirling down-draughts which buffet standing crops and are uncomfortable for livestock.

Where land is in long-term fallow (set-aside) in response to a government scheme for reducing food production, there is a choice. Little harm is caused by not coppicing for the few years while the land is uncropped, but appropriate trees should be coppiced before the first crop, otherwise its yield may be adversely affected.

9.2 Blackthorn and Hawthorn

The thorns are the most obvious casualty of the 'short top and sides' slaughter of our hedges. Fortunately they survive, just, in those hedges which have been trimmed less assiduously. They host many species of insects and are the basic habitat for our hedgerow birds. In evolutionary terms, when traditionally managed with coppiced trees, their scrubby habitats resemble the ancient woodland edge. Although both Blackthorn and Hawthorn have thorns and grow in similar situations, they are only distantly related and are easily identified.

Blackthorn and Hawthorn

Blackthorn (Slone Tree, Sloe Tree) flowers on the bare branches, before

September, and farmers are recommended to urge MAFF for this exemption for their rotational land. For both rotational and non-rotational set-aside land, non-residual sprays applied by spot or wick are permitted. Application by wick is recommended as it selects the taller vigorous weeds, but it needs care to be effective.

A MAFF explanatory guide describes the Field Margin option as offering "considerable agronomic and environmental advantages. It minimises the disturbance to existing farming patterns, allows easier access to maintain features such as hedges and ditches and can be used to 'square up' irregular fields. At the same time it can provide new habitats and extend and link existing habitats, for example providing hunting grounds for barn owls."

8.2 Pasture Fields

The wise livestock farmer with permanent grass leaves a similar wildlife field margin unsprayed and unfertilised. In mowing for silage or hay, this strip is left uncut, thus speeding the operation and preventing much of the damage to the cutter-bar from stones dislodged from the hedge. In the autumn, the strip is topped off with the rest of the field. The all-grass farmer is not concerned with spraying off and ploughing his wildlife field margin and there are fewer plant species.

For silage fields the margins are essential refuges for wildlife in the month following each cut. The females of several butterflies including the Meadow Brown, Small Heath and Wall Brown lay their eggs on taller grass stems at various times during the summer. Uncut margins in silage fields are not heavily grazed during the summer months and therefore often provide an ideal habitat for these species (Fry & Lonsdale, 1991).

The autumn mowing or topping is best done at the height of 300mm (12") because of the need to provide a good winter habitat for predators e.g. insects and mice. In the years following ploughing, the unsown field margin produces a wide variety of flowering species which eventually become dominated by grasses. When the adjoining hedge is managed traditionally, the timing of when the margin should be refurbished is not critical .

This wildlife field margin in pasture is especially useful in avoiding waste of fertiliser spread on to the hedge, typified by lush growths of Nettle and Cleavers (Goosegrass) that smother the less vigorous plants. Autumn topping of the field margin allows for the seeding of most wild plants, while maintaining a habitat similar to a coarse hay-meadow. Larger animals use it as a corridor. Barn Owls traditionally hunt along hedge-lines but the main attraction is in the field margin by the hedge base where the tussocky vegetation is home for Voles and other prey. The establishment of wildlife field margins is bringing back many more of the owls and other birds of prey. Whether they, and other animals which live partly in or over hedges, should be listed as hedge dwellers is a question of definition. The important fact is that their numbers are seriously diminished when hedges are not traditionally managed.

8.3 Hedge Junctions

Where field hedges join there are usually tight corners where it is uneconomic to cultivate. These make good wildlife field margins. Reversing implements into these corners to cultivate and tidy up is a waste of the farmer's money and he loses an opportunity to increase the number of helpful predator species. On livestock farms, there is almost always space for a grazed but uncultivated, unfertilised triangle of tussocky and scrubby habitat in the corner of grazing fields. Even where the area is only a few square metres, livestock welcome the rough herbage, the shelter and dry-lying. On arable farms the corner is best totally neglected except for mowing a margin next to the cropped area, and for coppicing trees. The larger areas can support several coppiced trees without detriment to the crop. Where several field corners coincide, they combine to make a small copse which can be valuable for wildlife and landscape in the less wooded parts of Cornwall, and which is likely to host a large number of species to replenish nearby field hedges.

8.4 Ditches and Streams

The field ditch or stream alongside a hedge combines to become an even more valuable wildlife habitat. In Cornwall this is often best managed by allowing Bramble and other climbing and shrubby plants on the hedge-side to arch over the ditch, thus darkening its sides and bottom. Without light, the ditch stays unchoked by weeds, runs unimpeded for many years and is often favoured by Otters. The field margin beside the ditch is usually at least 2m (6') wide, perhaps fenced, to provide stability to the ditch side. Thus the effective width of the hedge is trebled with a habitat much enhanced by the damp conditions in the ditch with its scrubby cover. The real value is increased when the hedge itself is managed traditionally.

Less common is the hedge with a stream at its base which meanders slightly so that there is an irregular margin of land between the hedge and stream; here the extra width is especially useful for wildlife, including the Common Wren , an avid aphid feeder (Pollard et al., 1974). Small areas of marsh or bog are often in low-lying field corners. Today it is seldom economic to drain them. As they are vital to many helpful and now-protected species such as the Frog, they should be left as rough grazing. In an arable field, a wide margin should be left between the boggy area and the drier ground. Hedges next to these areas should be allowed to overgrow completely as they will not affect production.

Hedge Bindweed

9.

TREATMENT OF HEDGEROW TREES

In Cornwall, hedgerow trees were often more prominent than woodland trees before the advent of Dutch Elm disease, mechanical hedge trimming and forestry grants. In addition to being a significant landscape component, they serve as hosts for many relic woodland species and as wildlife corridors between woods.

Mature hedgerow trees cause practical problems to the structure of a Cornish hedge. Maclean (1992) quotes William Pontey, in The Forest Pruner (1805), as being clearly against the abundance of trees in an English hedgerow and offering a long list of reasons which are as valid today as 200 years ago. With stone and Cornish hedges, the roots of large trees penetrate along the hedge, expand against the stones and gradually dislodge them. Eventually each uncoppiced tree starts to die, is wind-blown and its uprooted stump makes a large cavity in the hedge and loosens many stones around. Traditionally Cornish farmers were aware of this and, appreciating the shelter given by trees, practised selective coppicing.

The angled cut of the hedge-top with the flail as described in Chapter 6 encourages the selection and retention of stool growth in native and naturalised trees along the centre line of hedge. Preventing trees from growing out of the side of the hedge preserves its structure and optimises dappled shade on the hedge top and sides. The new tree growths, together with planted trees, on hedge-tops must be coppiced when they grow big enough. Unfortunately ignorant excessive use of mechanical trimmers operates against this. One result of the 'short-top-and-sides' is that many of our hedgerow trees are reduced to grotesque living tree stumps. These cast too much bottom shade and make a weakness in the hedge. In fairness, most of the present generation of farmers have had little actual experience of traditional practice.

9.1 Coppicing

In Cornwall most broad-leaved trees, especially Sycamore, readily regrow from a 300mm (12") high stump. The stool tends to grow small roots because there is little demand for trunk anchorage from winds, and the tree's life is prolonged indefinitely. Trees are traditionally coppiced before the trunk is *"as thick as a man's thigh at breast height"*. At this size, about 250mm (10") diameter at 1.2m (4') high, the trunk and branches are removed easily without damaging the hedge. The size of the leaves emerge, in March/April over several weeks which usually coincide with a spell of cold weather with Arctic winds, thus the term "Blackthorn Winter". It grows as a thicket to a height of 3m (10ft) and has small oval leaves and blackish bark. Its small edible, but astringent, plum-like fruits are the sloes of sloe-gin (old saying: "as dry as slone pastry" Davey, 1909). Blackthorn has no need of coppicing as it immortalises and spreads itself by producing suckers, a distinct advantage not always appreciated when it spreads into naturalised pastures.

Hawthorn (May, Quick, Whitethorn) blooms after the leaves have emerged in April/May, sometimes overlapping with Blackthorn. Its flowering usually coincides with the British spring, hence the saying: "Ne'er cast a clout e'er May is out", in other words, not to discard one's winter vest until the Hawthorn has finished blooming. It grows as a single tree to a height of 5m (16ft), has three- or five-lobed leaves and grey bark, and the fruits are small bunches of red haws (Cornish: aglets, Davey 1909). Hawthorn is a relatively short lived tree but it rejuvenates readily after being coppiced when about 150mm (6") diameter at breast height, or cut-and-laid.

The cutting-and-laying of Hawthorn is often practised in East Cornwall with turf hedges that are low and tend towards the ordinary thorn hedge found in other parts of Britain. On Cornish hedges where there is a gap in the shrubby cover, often a Hawthorn branch is half-cut and bent over on to the earth and anchored by a stone. Soil and turf is cast up from the base of the hedge on to the twiggy end of the branch to ensure that it roots into the hedge-top and starts another bush or tree.

Both thorns sculpture magnificently when constantly exposed to the salt winds in Cornwall, when their eventual heights are much lower and reached at greater age.

9.3 Planting trees on hedges

The main planting of trees on new hedges should be Blackthorn. Although the young plants may be twice as costly as Hawthorn, it is more tolerant of salt-laden gales and, because of its suckering habit, can be planted at a third of the density of Hawthorn. Blackthorn still attracts about two-thirds of the animal species associated with Hawthorn, and it is a better foundation for Cornish hedges. Other local tree species should be planted at the same time at an irregular spacing of about 5-10m (5-10yds). These should be Oak, Ash, Elm, Sycamore and/or Hawthorn with occasional Holly, Gorse and Sallow according to local circumstance, but not the other species advised by ADAS (Berryman. 1993).

For new hedges not on farms, Gorse is useful because of its attractive flowers and resistance against vandalism, and only needs trimming every few years. Western Gorse is more manageable than the European Gorse; neither tolerates vigorous weed competition when newly planted. There is a crying need for Blackthorn and Western Gorse seedlings from native Cornish stock to be commercially available for new hedges. Maclean (1992) advises Sea Buckthorn for exposed maritime conditions but it is a foreign species without dependant fauna, is overly costly, and its suckering is too aggressive; it is therefore not recommended.

The planting of trees on existing Cornish hedges is difficult because of dry soil and root competition, and is usually unnecessary. The majority of hedges already contain tree seedlings occurring naturally which need only to be allowed to develop. Young trees may be planted in those hedges devoid of tree species, but need extra care during establishment. Although some 40 tree species have been recorded on Cornish hedges (CBRU), only the local species listed above which are amenable to coppicing should be planted. There is no justification for planting tree species other than those occurring naturally in Cornish hedges. Each new non-local species brings conditions for its own attendant wildlife which alter the delicate balance of native species. Fortunately the Thorns, Elm, Ash and the relative newcomer Sycamore are still widespread and only need encouragement by enlightened trimming to re-establish themselves. Sessile Oak, with the large, heavy and stalk-less acorn, should be planted preferentially. Although regulations discourage trade in local seed, ways should be made to ensure that local strains of oak are planted. Acorns are easily germinated in a sand box kept over winter (on a roof away from mice) and grown on for two years in a garden before planting with a tube/mat on a hedge.

When planted or naturally-occurring saplings reach about 5m (15ft) they should be coppiced at about 0.6m (2'); otherwise they will increasingly reduce crop yields, sway in the wind and rack (destabilise) the hedge with their roots, especially in windy spots.

9.4 Maturing trees

Trees should always be allowed to develop to maturity when in copses, bottoms, field corners or other situations where the integrity of a hedge is not involved. Sometimes occasional mature trees and amenity avenues of Beech and other species are so valuable as to merit the extra work in maintaining their associated hedges.
Allowing over-mature trees to become dangerously unsafe before felling is an unwise temptation. Identified by being hollow or 'stag-headed',

over-mature trees are felled with as tall a stump as is safe at that location, preferably at a height of 3m-4m (9ft-12ft). There is often regeneration. If the tree is dying, the stump will take 10-20 years to rot; and in the meanwhile it provides an invaluable habitat for fungi and the larval stage of many insects. As wood is very indigestible, insects often need fungi to have started the job; some, such as the ambrosia beetles, actually take their special fungus with them to new breeding sites (Fry & Lonsdale, 1991).

Clad with Ivy, these tall stumps give roost and nesting sites to birds and late-summer nectar to insects. Typically as the stump is gradually consumed by wildlife, it is held upright by the all-embracing Ivy; eventually toppling over with so little remaining substance that the hedge structure is not further damaged.

Turf Hedge

10.

CONTROL OF RABBITS IN CORNISH HEDGES

Most of our hedges were built long before the Normans spread rabbits across Britain via artificial warrens. The successful long term future of the Cornish hedge depends on preventing rabbits from becoming as numerous as in pre-myxomatosis days. Despite the beneficial effect their browsing has for some plant and insect species, their numbers must be controlled in order to preserve the hedge structure. Careful attention to hedge maintenance is the best way of preventing rabbits from establishing themselves.

One of the reasons for trimming hedges is the discouragement of rabbits. With a stone or Cornish hedge in good repair, the only way to dig a burrow into the hedge is from the top. This means that when the rabbit travels to and from the feeding area in the field, it has to go down and up the side of the hedge, exposing itself to predators. The old people always said that a reasonably trimmed Cornish or stone hedge with tight sides and an open top sufficiently discouraged the invasion of rabbits so that the odd hole started in the top was easy to deal with; the entrances were filled in with stones and a sod and stamped down. Today rabbit infiltration more often starts on the side of the hedge near its base where a stone has been torn out by flailing or displaced by subsidence, erosion, livestock or tree root.

Already there are increasing populations in some localities, causing farmers much anxiety, and the problem worsens as rabbits become cyclically host-tolerant to myxomatosis. Traditional methods, eg lamping, ferrets, long nets, are used by farmers and others for enjoyment and do reduce rabbit numbers but are seldom economic. Most existing methods of controlling rabbits tend to be of localised or temporary benefit. Gassing or fencing is effective only when carried out properly. Enlightened research is required.

A good reason for traditional rabbit-catching is that unrestricted infestation leads inexorably towards an urge for more hedge-removal instead of proper maintenance. In earlier days on the better farms, hedges which were badly honeycombed, with much of the core of the hedge excavated out into the field, were rebuilt section by section over the years. On other farms they were left to run down and become a nondescript scrub-covered line of stones and earth with little visual semblance of the original hedge; their repair became uneconomic. Whilst excellent habitats, these are no barrier for stock and require good fencing. Nevertheless they should be kept; in some cases government grant may assist in reinstatement.

Always the argument for the removal of these untidy heaps, because they are no longer proper hedges, should be firmly resisted. Fenced tight on both sides with barbed wire and perhaps netting, trimming outside the fence will gradually produce a reasonable field boundary despite the rabbits. Not usually appreciated is the valuable harbourage which is given by these wilder habitats to the natural predators of the rabbit. The gin trap disproportionately reduced the weasel population which may return as rabbits multiply (Torr, 1921).

Although the actual structure of some Cornish hedges may be ruinous, their ancient presence in the landscape needs to be preserved.

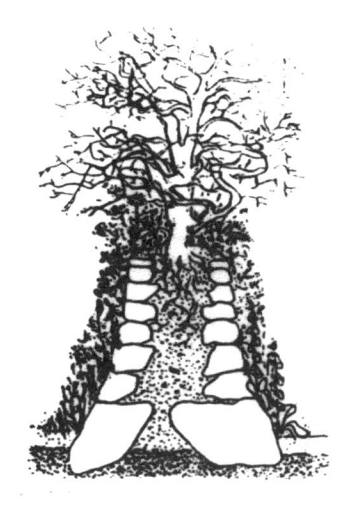

Cornish Hedge

11.

ROADSIDE HEDGES, LEGAL OBLIGATIONS AND SPECIAL NEEDS

No longer does the parish roadman with intimate knowledge of his stretches of road restrict his summer trimming to the blind corners and other needs of traffic safety, leaving most of the hedge trimming to the winter months. Those days of hand work have gone, unlikely to return.

However the Cornwall County Council is very conscious of the beauty of the countryside, and obviously encourages hedge growth to be enjoyed by all for as long as possible. The Council's Environmental Charter makes specific mention of its policy towards hedge-trimming, use of pesticides, tree planting and the maintenance of flora and fauna. This booklet sets out the technical background necessary for the implementation of this Charter in respect of the care of roadside hedges.

Trimming is required in accordance with section 154 of the Highways Act 1980 and places the duty on the occupier/landowner. This obligation applies to all registered rights of way, including byways, bridleways and footpaths, although trimming may have been done by the County Council in the past. There will be occasions when landowners will be required to trim a roadside hedge, perhaps outside of the ideal times, to ensure the safe passage of the travelling public. During the growing season some annual growth may need more than a single cut up to 2 metres in height, but the higher growth up to 5.1 metres high is trimmed only between the start of November and the end of February.

In the long-term interests of road safety and hedge structure, new roadside Cornish hedges should be top-planted with Blackthorn, not Hawthorn, at 1m (1yd) apart, twice the interval of Hawthorn.

Young trees are coppiced and over-mature trees are felled when becoming liable to be wind-blown on to the road. This Guidance note gives technical advice which more than doubles the number of flowering hedge plant species, as compared with annual summer trimming. Occupiers/landowners seeking to trim their roadside hedges in accordance with this Guidance note should categorise them :-

Category A   Hedges on blind corners, road junctions etc. where sight-lines need to be unobstructed at all times during the year. These short sections of hedge on any width of highway are trimmed to 200-300mm (8"-12") at the end of May and again at the end of July. Some exceptions may be made of little-frequented narrow single-lane roads that, for example, lead only to farms.

Category B Hedges on all roads where there is sufficient verge for one pass of the Highways flail. The remainder of the verge and the hedge is trimmed by the farmer once every 3 years on a rotational basis with about a third of this length trimmed each year so as to preserve a seeding cycle for annuals, excepting where bramble growth tip-roots annually into the verge (instead of being weathered-back by wind) when trimming is every 2 years, with about a half done each year.

Category C Hedges on two-lane roads more than 18ft. wide (with a central white road marking) where hedges arise from the edge of the tarmac (i.e. there is no verge). Trimming is done once each year and only between the start of November and the end of February.

Category D Hedges on two-lane roads of less than 18ft wide (and no central white road marking). Where the hedges rise vertically from the edge of the tarmac, except where the road is little-frequented, these hedges are trimmed twice a year in June and in August. Otherwise the hedges are trimmed once each year and only between the start of November and the end of February.

Category E Hedges on single-lane roads where meeting traffic uses passing-places. Each passing-place is trimmed twice a year in June and August; the rest is trimmed once a year and only between the start of November and the end of February.

Category **A** hedges should be trimmed no closer than 200mm (8"), but no longer than 300mm (12"). Tighter cutting takes longer, dislodges hedging stones on to the highway which may cause an accident, and more severely reduces the wildlife.

Categories **B** and **C** should be winter-trimmed to leave about 250mm-500mm (12"-20") growth, so as to preserve best the hedge structure.

Categories **D** and **E** should be summer-trimmed to leave 300-500 mm (12"-20") growth on the hedge; in other words, no more than a skim-cut to remove tall and woody species such as Cow Parsley, Bracken and Bramble, whilst leaving the less vigorous flowers in bloom. An easy way is to trim off the tall white flowers, and leave the shorter blue, red, and/or yellow flowers, whichever is in bloom at the time. The main winter cut should be at 200-300mm (8"-12").

Probably 80% of roadside hedges fall easily within these relevant categories; thus making this standard of management a good target to aim for over a period of years. However there are often, on roads of Categories **C** - **E**, some blind corners and other places where safety is impaired and a short length of Category **A** trimming is required. Farmers must resist the temptation to treat long lengths of hedge as Category **A** when frequent trimming is needed. Over-trimming is more costly for the farmer and seriously damages the wild-life.

Situations of dense shade, or of windswept or sea exposure, require less than average trimming. Similarly stone hedges need little or no trimming. In these cases, farmers should use a less demanding category according to the circumstance.

The least demanding Category **B** hedges, in sheltered areas of Cornwall, are likely to contain 150-200 species of flowering broad-leaved plants within a typical mile. Conversely the most demanding Category **A** will probably contain, after several years of trimmings, less than 50 species even in sheltered areas. In the interests of economics and conservation, farmers should choose the least demanding category appropriate to the needs of the highway.

If in any doubt, farmers should consult the Highways Department of Cornwall County Council which is always ready to help in deciding the categories for the various parts of the road-side hedges.

REFERENCES & APPENDICES
References.

Allaby M. (1981). *A Year in the Life of a Field.* David & Charles, Newton Abbott.

Almond W.E. (1975). *The Distribution of Bumblebees in Cornwall and the Isles of Scilly.* Cornish Studies, 3: 5-18.

Barker D. (1986). *Hoverflies of a Sheviock Valley.* Caradon Field & Nat. Hist. Club Ann. Report 1986: 31

Bere R. (1982). *The Nature of Cornwall.* Barracuda Books, Buckingham.

Berryman A. (1993). *Management Guidelines for Hedgerows and Hedgerow Trees.* Agricultural Developement and Advisory Service, Exeter.

Carrington E. (1898). *The Farmer and the Birds.* George Bell & Sons, London.

Carter S. (1985). *Hedge Flails - A Disaster for Cornwall.* Community News. Summer 1985: 8-9. Cornwall Rural Community Council, Truro.

Carter S. (1986). *The Disaster of the Hedge Flail.* The Lizard 3 & 4: 16-21.

Coleman-Cooke J. (1965). *The Harvest that Kills.* Odham Books, London.

Davey Hamilton F. (1909). *Flora of Cornwall.* Chegwidden, Penryn.

Dowdeswell W.H. (1987). *Hedgerows and Verges.* Allen & Unwin, London.

Fry R. & Lonsdale D (ed.) (1991). *Habitat Conservation for Insects - A Neglected Green Issue.* The Amateur Entomologists' Society, Middlesex.

Humphreys J. (1980). *The land and freshwater mollusca of St. Ives, Cornwall. Part 1: shell-bearing species.* J. Conch Lond., 30: 155-166.

Keble Martin W. (1965). *The Concise British Flora in Colour.* George Rainbird, London.

Johnson J. (1993). *Working Together.* Countryside, 60: 3.

Johnson J. & Rose P. (1994). *Bodmin Moor. An Archaeological Survey. Vol 1 The Human Landscape.* English Heritage, London.

Maclean M. (1992). *New Hedges for the Countryside.* Farming Press Books, Ipswich.

MAFF (1993). *Arable Area Payments 1993/4. Explanatory Guide.* Ministry of Agriculture, Fisheries & Food, London.

Margetts L.J. & David R.W. (1981). *A Review of the Cornish Flora.* Board of Agriculture and Internal Improvement, London.

Margetts L.J. & Spurgin K.L. (1991). *The Cornish Flora Supplement (1981-1990)*. Trendrine Press, Zennor.
Massee A.M. (1955). *The County Distribution of the British Hemiptera Heteroptera. Second edition*. Entom. mon. Mag. 91: 7-27.
McCartney P. (1993). *Birds & Hedgerows*. Unpublished Report. CTNC, Allet, Truro.
Murphy R.J. (1985). *Hedges, Reskadinnick, Camborne*. Unpublished Report. Available from Inst. Cornish Studies, Pool, Redruth.
Nance, Morton R. (1978). *An English-Cornish and Cornish-English Dictionary*. The Cornish Language Board, Penzance.
Novák I. (1985). *A Field Guide to Butterflies and Moths*. Octopus Books, London.
Paton J.A. (1969). *A Bryophyte Flora of Cornwall*. Trans. British Bryological Soc. 5: 669-756.
Paton J.A. (1981). *Wild Flowers in Cornwall*. Bradford Barton, Truro.
Pay A.R. (1993). *St Keverne Group Conservation Scheme, Survey of Breeding Birds 1991-92*. Unpublished. Cornwall Farming and Wildlife Advisory Group, Truro.
Pollard E., Hooper M.D. & Moore N.W. (1974). *Hedges*. New Naturalist series. Collins, London.
Stace C.A. (1990). *New flora of the British Isles*. St. Edmundsbury Press, St. Edmunds, Suffolk.
Stubbs A.E. & Falk S.J. (1983). *British Hoverflies*. Brit. Ent. Nat. Hist. Soc., London.
Torr C. (1921). *Small Talk at Wreyland*. Cambridge University Press.
Whitlock, Ralph (1985).*The Oak*. George Unwin, Hemel Hempstead, Herts.
Wratten S. (1993). *Helping Nature To Control Pests*. Game Conservancy, Fordingbridge, Hants.
Worgan, G.B. (1811). *General View of the Agriculture of the County of Cornwall*. Board of Agriculture and Internal Improvement, London. Agriculture, Fisheries & Food, London.

Appendix A

FLOWERING PLANTS & FERNS FOUND BY SARAH CARTER IN TWO MILES OF ROADSIDE HEDGE AT SANCREED DURING THE PERIOD 1970-1993.

The subject area is one mile of a single-track road near Sancreed Churchtown west of Penzance and typical of very many in Cornwall. The lane traverses a southern slope, going from 120m up to 140m and down to 120m above sea level. Half of the lane runs southwest, the other half southeast. The less typical species and casuals were close to the site of a late-Mediæval roadside cottage.

Carter began observation of these hedges in 1960 continuing, through the period of summer flail cutting 1972-89, to date. Plants noticeably flowering during 1971 in both hedges along the mile of minor road are listed below together with the subsequent years of occurrence. Ferns and shrubby species were included; grasses were excluded.

Moth and butterfly food plants shown in upper case (MB) are those identified by Spalding as being the preferred food of the larvae of butterflies and moths that are likely to be found in hedges throughout Cornwall. The greater number shewn in lower-case (mb) are those plants that, in Carter's experience of hedges in West Cornwall, may be eaten by caterpillars, depending on other environmental factors, and include non-preferred plants.

Common and scientific names follow Stace, 1990 with some Cornish names in brackets (Nance, 1978).

KEY:-   a/b=annual & biennial; p=perennial; rd=Red Data Book; M/B=foodplant for moth/butterfly (Spalding, 1993); mb=foodplant for moth/butterfly (Carter, 1994).
*=flowering; blind=not flowering; r=seriously reduced; e=endangered lost=absent; c=comeback; i=increasing; a=rampant. s = scarce

HEDGE PLANTS - YEARS OF OCCURRANCE

1971		1974	/78	/85	/93
Agrimony, *Agrimonia eupatoria*, p	m	*r	*e	lost	
Agrimony, Hemp (Scawen dhu)					
Eupatorium cannabinum, p	m	*r	blind	lost	
Angelica, Wild *Angelica sylvestris*, p	m	blind	blind	blind	*s

HEDGE PLANTS - YEARS OF OCCURRANCE

1971		1974	/78	/85	/93
Avens, Common, *Geum urbanum,* p	m	*	*r	lost	
Bartsia, Yellow, *Parentucellia viscosa,* a	mb	*e	lost		
Bedstraw, Heath, *Galium saxatile,* p M	m	*	*	*r	*
Bedstraw, Hedge, *Galium mollugo,* p	m	*	*r	*e	*
Bedstraw, Lady's, *Galium verum,* p M	m	lost			
Betony (Les-Dosak) *Stachys officinalis,* p	m	*	*r	*e	*i
Bindweed, Hedge, *Calystegia sepium,* p	m	*r	lost		c
Bindweed, Large, *Calystegia sylvatica,* p	m	*	blind	blind	*
Bird's-foot, *Ornithopus perpusillus,* p	mb	*e	lost		
Bittersweet, *Solanum dulcamara,* p	m	*e	lost		
Blackthorn (Dren, Spernen dhu, Yrynen)					
Prunus spinosa, p	m	*	*r	*r	*
Bluebell (Blejen an Gok)					
*Hyacinthoides non-scripta,*p	M	*	*	blind	*
Bracken (Redenen)					
Pteridium aquifolium, pM	m	*	*a	*a	*
Bramble (Dreysen) *Rubus fruticosus agg.,* p	m	blind	blind	blind	*
Broom, *Cytisus scoparius,* p M/B	mb	*r	blind	lost	
Bryony, Black, *Tamus communis,* p		*e	lost		
Bugle, *Ajuga reptans,* p	m	*	*e	lost	
Burdock, *Arctium minus group,* b	mb	*r	*e	lost	
Buttercup, Creeping, *Ranunculus repens,* p		*	*r	*r	*i
Buttercup, Meadow, *Ranunculus acris,* p		*e	lost		
Butterfly Bush, *Buddleia davidii,* p		*	*	*	*
Campion, Red, *Silene dioica,* p M	m	*r	*r	*r	*i
Campion, hybrid, *Silene dioica x latifolia,* p,	m	*r	*e	lost	
Campion, White, *Silene latifolia,* p M	m	*e	lost		
Carrot, Wild (Caretysen)					
*Daucus carota ssp.carota,*p m		*	blind	r	*s
Cat's-ear, *Hypochaeris radicata,* p	m	*	*r	*r	*i
Celandine, Lesser (Losow lagas)					
*Ranunculus ficaria,*p		*	*	*	*
Chervil, Rough,					
Chaerophyllum temulentum, p	m	*r	*e	lost	c
Chickweed, Common, *Stellaria media,* a	m	*	*r	*e	lost
Cinquefoil, Creeping, *Potentilla reptans,* p	m	*	*	*r	*
Cleavers (Split) *Galium aparine,* a M	m	*	r	r	*i
Clover, Red (Mullyonen)					
Trifolium pratense, p M/B	mb	*r	*e	lost	

HEDGE PLANTS - YEARS OF OCCURRANCE

1971		1974	/78	/85	/93
Clover, White (Mullyonen)					
Trifolium repens, p M/B	mb	*	*	*	*
Crane's-bill, Cut-leaved,					
Geranium dissectum, a	m	*r	*e	*e	*i
Crane's-bill, Dove's-foot, *Geranium molle*, a	m	*	*r	*e	*s
Crane's-bill, Hedgerow,					
Geranium pyrenaicum, p	m	*	*e	lost	
Crane's-bill, Small-flowered,					
Geranium pusillum, a	m	*e	lost		
Creeping Jenny, *Lysimachia nummularia*, p		*r	*e	lost	
Cress, Hairy Bitter, *Cardamine hirsuta*, a		*	*	*	*
Cuckoo-flower, *Cardamine pratensis*, p	b	*	*r	*e	*s
Daffodil (Afodyl, Lylyen-Cirawys)					
Narcissus cv., p		*	blind	blind	*s
Daisy, Oxeye (Caja vras)					
Leucanthemum vulgare, p		*e	lost		
Daisy (Ygor) *Bellis perennis*, p		*	*	*r	*
Dandelion (Dans-lew)					
Taraxacum vulgare, p	m	*	*	*r	*
Dead-nettle, Red (Coklynasen ruth)					
Lamium purpureum, a	m	*e	lost		
Dead-nettle, Spotted (Coklynasen)					
Lamium maculatum, p	m	*r	*e	lost	
Dead-nettle, White (Coklynasen wyn)					
Lamium album,p	m	*e	lost		
Dock, Broad-leaved (Tavolen)					
Rumex obtusifolius,p	mb	*	blind	r	*
Dock, Curled, *Rumex crispus*, p	mb	*	blind	r	*
Dock, Wood (Tavol) *Rumex sanguineus*, p	mb	*	*r	lost	
Elder (Scawen) *Sambucus nigra*, p		*r	*r	lost	
Eyebright, *Euphrasia sp.*, a	m	*	*e	lost	
Fern, Broad Buckler, *Dryopteris dilatata*, p		*r	*r	*e	*i
Fern, Hart's-tongue,					
Phyllitis scolopendrium, p		*r	*r	*e	*
Fern, Lady, *Athyrium filix-femina*, p		*	*r	*e	*
Fern, Male (Redenen) *Dryopteris filix-mas*, p		*r	*r	*e	*i
Fern, Mountain Male, *Dryopteris oreades*, p		*r	*e	*e	*
Fern, Scaly Male, *Dryopteris pseudomas*, p		*	*r	*e	*

HEDGE PLANTS - YEARS OF OCCURRANCE

		1971		1974	/78	/85	/93
Fern, Polypody, *Polypodium vulgare* group, p				*	*	*	*
Figwort, Common, *Scrophularia nodosa*, p			m	blind	blind	blind	*s
Figwort, Water, *Scrophularia auriculata*, p			m	blind	blind	blind	*s
Fleabane, Common, *Pulicaria dysenterica*, p			m	blind	e	lost	
Forget-me-not, Field (Scorpyonles)							
Mysotis arvensis, p			m	*	*r	*e	*s
Foxglove (Manek-lowarn)							
Digitalis purpurea, b			m	*r	*e	*e	*i
Fumitory, Common, *Fumaria officinalis*, a				lost			
Fumitory, Common Ramping, *Fumaria muralis*							
ssp. *boraei*, a				*e	blind	lost	cs
Fumitory, Purple Ramping, *Fumaria purpurea*, a				*e	lost		
Fumitory, Tall Ramping, *Fumaria bastardii*, a				*e	blind	lost	cs
Fumitory, Western Ramping, *Fumaria occidentalis*, a				*e	lost		
Gladiolus, Eastern ('Jacks') *Gladiolus communis*							
ssp. *byzantinus*, p				lost			cs
Goldenrod, *Solidago virgaurea*, p			m	*r	blind	e	*s
Gorse, Western (Eythynen-dof) *Ulex gallii*, p			mb	*	*r	*r	*i
Gorse (Eythynen-Frynk) *Ulex europaeus*, p			mb	*	*r	*r	*i
Ground-elder, *Aegopodium podagraria*, p			m	blind	lost		
Ground-ivy (Ydhyowen)							
Glechoma hederacea, p			m	*	*r	*e	lost
Groundsel (Madere) *Senecio vulgaris*, a			m	*r	*e	*e	*s
Hawkbit, Autumn *Leontodon autumnalis*, p				*	*r	*e	lost
Hawkbit, Hairy, *Leontodon taraxacoides*, p				*	*r	lost	
Hawksbeard, Beaked, *Crepis vesicaria*, p			m	*r	*e	lost	c
Hawks-beard, Smooth, *Crepis capillaris*, a			m	*r	*r	*r	*i
Hawkweed, Umbellate, *Hieracium umbellatum*, p	*			*r	*r	*i	
Hawthorn (Dren, Speren wyn)							
Crataegus monogyna, p			m	*	*r	*e	*i
Heath, Cross-leaved, *Erica tetralix*, p				*r	*e	lost	
Heather (Gruk) *Calluna vulgaris*, p M			m	*r	*e	lost	
Heather, Bell, *Erica cinerea*, p			m	*	*r	*e	*
Heliotrope, Winter, *Petasites fragrans*, p				*	*a	*a	*
Hemp-nettle, Common, *Galeopsis tetrahit* a			m	*r	lost		
Herb-Robert, *Geranium robertianum*, a				*r	*e	*e	*i
Hogweed (Panesen)							
Heracleum sphondylium, p			m	*	blind	r	*

65

HEDGE PLANTS - YEARS OF OCCURRANCE

1971		1974	/78	/85	/93
Holly (Kelynen) *Ilex aquifolium*, p B	b	*	*r	*r	*
Honeysuckle (Gwythvosen)					
Lonicera periclymenum, p	m	blind	blind	r	*
Ivy (Ydhyowen)					
Hedera helix hibernica, p M/B	mb	*	*a	*a	*
Knapweed, Greater (Pederow-pronter)					
Centauria scabiosa, p	m	*e	lost		
Knapweed, Lesser, *Centaurea nigra*, p	m	*r	blind	blind	*
Knotgrass, *Polygonum aviculare*, a	m	*	*r	lost	c
Knotweed, Japanese, *Fallopia japonica*, p		*	*a	*a	*
Leek, Three-cornered (gothkenynen)					
Allium triquetrum, p		*	*	*	*
Lords-and-ladies, Italian, *Arum italicum*, p		*	*	blind	*
Lords-and-ladies,					
Arum italicum ssp neglectum, p		*	*	blind	*
Madder, Wild, *Rubia peregrina*, p	m	lost			
Mallow, Common, *Malva sylvestris*, b	m	*e	lost		
Mayweed, Scentless (Fenokel cun)					
Tripleurospermum inodorum, a		*e	lost		
Medick, Black, *Medicago lupulina*, a	mb	*	*r	*e	lost
Medick, Spotted, *Medicago arabica*, a B	mb	*	*r	lost	
Milkwort, Heath, *Polygala serpyllifolia*, p		*r	lost		
Montbretia, *Crocosmia x crocosmiflora*, p		*	blind	r	*
Mouse-ear, Common, *Cerastium fontanum*					
ssp. *glabrescens*, a	m	*	*r	*r	*
Mouse-ear, Sticky, *Cerastium glomeratum*, a	m	*	*r	*r	*
Mugwort (Losles) *Artemesia vulgaris*, p M	m	blind	e	lost	
Mullein, Great, *Verbascum thapsus*, b	m	*e	lost		
Mustard, Black, *Brassica nigra*, a	b	*r	lost		cs
Mustard, Garlic (Kedhow)					
Alliaria petiolata, a	mb	*e	lost		
Mustard, Hedge (Kedhow)					
Sisymbrium officinale,a, B,	mb	*r	lost		
Navelwort, *Umbilicus rupestris*, p		*	*	*	*
Nettle (Lynasen) *Urtica dioica*, p M/B	mb	*	blind	r	*
Nightshade, Black (Morel)					
Solanum nigrum, a		*e	lost		
Nightshade, Enchanter's, *Circaea lutetiana*, p		*r	*e	lost	

HEDGE PLANTS - YEARS OF OCCURRANCE

1971		1974	/78	/85	/93
Nipplewort, *Lapsana communis*, a	m	*r	blind	e	*i
Orchid, Early-Purple, *Orchis mascula*, p		lost			
Orchid, Heath Spotted,					
Dactylorhiza maculata, p		*e	lost		
Pansy, Field, *Viola arvensis*, a	mb	*e	lost		
Pansy, Wild, *Viola tricolor*, a/b	mb	lost			
Parsley, Cow, *Anthriscus sylvestris*, p	m	*	*	*r	*
Parsley, Fool's, *Aethusa cynapium*, a		*r	*e	lost	
Pignut (Keleren) *Conopodium majus*, p M	m	*	*	*	*
Pimpernel, Scarlet (Brathles)					
Anagallis arvensis, a		*r	lost		
Pineapple Weed, *Matricaria discoidea*, a		*	*r	lost	c
Plantain, Great, *Plantago major*, p	m	*	*r	lost	c
Plantain, Ribwort (Ladan-les)					
Plantago lanceolata, p, M	m	*	*	*r	*
Primrose (Bryallen) *Primula vulgaris*, p	m	*	*	*e	lost
Privet, Wild, *Ligustrum vulgare*, p	m	*r	*e	lost	
Ragwort (Madere bras) *Senecio jacobaea*, p	m	*	*r	lost	cs
Redshank, *Persicaria maculosa*, a		*r	lost		
Rose, Burnet, *Rosa pimpinellifolia*, p	m	blind	blind	blind	*
Rose, Dog (Rosen) *Rosa canina*, p M	m	blind	blind	lost	cs
Rose, Field (Rosen) *Rosa arvensis*, p	m	blind	blind	lost	
Rush, Soft, *Juncus effusus*, p		*	*	*r	*i
Sage, Wood, *Teucrium scorodonia*, p	m	*	*	*r	*i
St John's Wort, Slender,					
Hypericum pulchrum, p	m	*e	lost		cs
Scabious, Devil's-bit (Pen-glas)					
Succisa pratensis, p	m	*r	blind	blind	*s
Scabious, Field (Pen-glas)					
Knautia arvensis, p	m	*r	*e	lost	
Scabious, Sheep's-bit (Pen-glas)					
Jasione montana, p Mm		*	*	*r	*
Sedge, Pendulous, *Carex pendula*, p M	m	*	*	*	*
Self-heal, *Prunella vulgaris*, p		*r	blind	lost	
Silverweed, *Potentilla anserina*, p		*	*r	lost	c
Sorrel, Common, *Rumex acetosa*, p	mb	*	*	*	*
Sorrel, Sheep's, *Rumex acetosella*, p	mb	*	*	*r	*i

HEDGE PLANTS - YEARS OF OCCURRANCE

1971		1974	/78	/85	/93
Sorrel,Wood (Bara an gok) *Oxalis acetosella*, p		*e	lost		
Sow-thistle, Prickly (Losowen leth)					
Sonchus asper,a/b		*r	*e	lost	c
Sow-thistle, Smooth, *Sonchus oleraceus* a/b		*r	*e	lost	c
Speedwell, Common Field, *Veronica persica*, a	m	*	*r	*r	*
Speedwell, Germander, *Veronica chamaedrys*, p	m	*	*r	*r	*i
Speedwall, Slender, *Veronica filiformis*, p	m	*	*r	lost	
Speedwell, Thyme-leaved, *Veronica serpyllifolia*, p		*	*e	lost	
Spleenwort, Black, *Asplenium adiantum-nigrum*, p		*	*	*r	*s
Stitchwort, Greater, *Stellaria holostea*, p	m	*	*r	*e	*i
Stitchwort, Lesser, *Stellaria graminea*, p	m	*r	*e	lost	c
Stonecrop, English (Bewles) *Sedum anglicum*, a		*	*r	lost	cs
Strawberry, Barren (Pympdelen)					
Potentilla sterilis, p	m	*r	*e	lost	
Strawberry, Wild, *Fragaria vesca*, p	m	*	*e	lost	
Thistle, Creeping, *Cirsium arvense*, p	mb	*r	e	e	*s
Thistle, Spear, *Cirsium vulgare*, p	mb	*r	e	e	*s
Thyme, Wild, *Thymus polytrichus*, p	m	*e	lost		
Toadflax, Common, *Linaria vulgaris*, p	m	*e	lost		
Toadflax, Ivy-leaved, *Cymbalaria muralis*, p		*r	*e	lost	
Tormentil, Common, *Potentilla erecta*, p	m	*r	*e	*e	*i
Trefoil, Common Bird's-foot (Mullyon melen)					
Lotus corniculatus, p	mb	*	*r	lost	cs
Trefoil, Greater Bird's-foot (Mullyon melen)					
Lotus pedunculatus, p	mb	*r	blind	blind	*i
Trefoil, Lesser Yellow, *Trifolium dubium*, a	mb	*	*r	lost	c
Vervain, *Verbena officinalis*, p		*r	*e	lost	
Vetch, Bush (Gwek) *Vicia sepium*, p	m	*e	lost		
Vetch, Common (Gwek) *Vicia sativa*, p	m	*e	lost		
Vetch, Kidney, *Anthyllis vulneraria*, p		*e	lost		
Vetch, Narrow-leaved, *Vicia sativa ssp. nigra*, a	m	*r	*e	*e	*i
Vetch, Tufted, *Vicia cracca*, p	mb	*r	*e	*e	*i
Vetch, Wood, *Vicia sylvatica*, p		lost			
Vetchling, Meadow, *Lathyrus pratensis*, p	mb	*e	lost		cs
Violet, Common Dog, *Viola riviniana*, p B	mb	*	*	*r	*
Violet, Sweet, *Viola odorata*, p B	mb	*	*r	lost	
Violet, White Sweet,					
V. odorata ssp. dumetorum, p	mb	*	*	*r	*i

HEDGE PLANTS - YEARS OF OCCURRANCE

	1971		1974	/78	/85	/93
Willow-herb, Broad-leaved,						
Epilobium montanum, p		m	*e	lost		
Willow-herb, Rosebay,						
Chamaenerion angustifolium, p, M		m	*	*	*	*
Woundwort, Hedge, *Stachys sylvatica*, p		m	*r	blind	e	*i
Woundwort, Marsh, *Stachys palustris*, p		m	*e	*e	lost	cs
Yarrow, *Achillea millifolium*, p		m	*	blind	r	*

Appendix B

BUTTERFLY SPECIES RECORDED BY SARAH CARTER AS BREEDING AND/OR ON THE WING IN TWO MILES OF ROADSIDE HEDGE AT SANCREED DURING THE PERIOD 1970-1993

The subject area was the same as that for the plant species recorded in Appendix A. Observations of butterflies were as caterpillars on plants in the hedge, or on the wing in the immediate vicinity of the hedge.

KEY: *=observed; r=reduced; s=scarce; i=increased since 1985.

	Years Observed 1971 /85 /93				Years Observed 1971 /85 /93		
Wall Brown	*	*r		Small White	*	*s	*i
Hedge Brown	*	*s	*i	Orange-tip	*		*s
Meadow Brown	*	*s		Green-veined White	*		
Ringlet	*	*s		Common Blue	*		*s
Grayling	*			Silver Studded Blue	*		*s
Speckled Wood	*	*s	*i	Holly Blue	*s		*s
Comma	*			Clouded Yellow	*		*r
Small Tortoiseshell	*	*r		Silver-washed Fritillary	*s		
Red Admiral	*	*r		Dark Green Fritillary	*		
Peacock	*	*r		Small Skipper	*		
Painted Lady	*	*r		Small Heath	*		
Large White	*	*r		Small Copper	*		*r

Appendix C

FLOWERING PLANTS AND GRASSES FOUND BY SARAH CARTER IN FIELDS ADJOINING THE ROADSIDE HEDGE AT SANCREED IN 1993.

The fields had been sprayed, cultivated, bulb planted and then undisturbed for one year. Only species growing within the cultivated area were recorded. The original habitat for these fields varied from sallow wetland to lowland heath, covering about 28 ha (70 acres) and bounded on one side by the road hedge featured in Appendix A.

Moth and butterfly food plants shown in upper case (MB) are those identified by A.Spalding as being the preferred food of the larvae of butterflies and moths that are likely to be found throughout Cornwall. Common and scientific names follow Stace, 1990, Cornish names in brackets after Morton Nance, 1978. Species not indented also occurred in the hedge.

a/b= annual/biennial;
p= perennial.
M/B= foodplant for moth/butterfly (n=28) Spalding (1993).
D= densely concentrated in most-cropped fields n=14).

P= persistent in most-cropped fields (n=17).
E= mainly or exclusively in least-cropped fields (n=71).
W= widespread in variable numbers in all fields (n=21).

PLANT SPECIES IN FIELDS.

  Bedstraw, Marsh, *Galium palustre,* p, M, E
  Bindweed, Black, *Fallopia convolvulus,* a, W
  Blinks, Water, *Montia fontana,* a, E
Bluebell (Blejen-an-gok) *Hyacinthoides non-scripta,* p, M, E
  Brassica juncea (B. nigra x rapa) a, W
Burdock, Lesser (Amanyn) *Arctium minus* group b, W
Buttercup, Creeping, *Ranunculus repens,* p, D
  Buttercup, Hairy, *Ranunculus sardous,* a, E
  Buttercup, Small-flowered, *Ranunculus parviflorus,* a, E
Campion, hybrid, *Silene diocia x latifolia,* p, E
Campion, Red, *Silene dioica,* p, E
Campion, White, *Silene latifolia,* p, M, E
Carrot, Wild, *Daucus carota ssp.carota,* p, E
Cat's-ear, *Hypochaeris radicata,* p, E
  Chamomile, Stinking, *Anthemis cotula,* a, E

PLANT SPECIES IN FIELDS.

Chickweed, Common, *Stellaria media,* a, D
  Cinquefoil, Sulphur (Pympdelen) *Potentilla recta,* p, E
Cleavers (Split) *Galium aparine,* a, M, D
  Clover, Alsike (Mullyonen) *Trifolium hybridum,* p, E
Clover, Red, *Trifolium pratense,* p, E
Clover, White (Mullyonen) *Trifolium repens,* p, M/B, D
Crane's-bill, Cut-leaved, *Geranium dissectum,* a, E
Crane's-bill, Dove's-foot, *Geranium molle,* a, E
Crane's-bill, Small-flowered, *Geranium pusillum,* a, E
Cress, Hairy Bitter, *Cardamine hirsuta,* a, W
  Cudweed, Marsh, *Gnaphalium uliginosum,* a, E
Daisy (Ygor) *Bellis perennis,* p, W
Daisy, Oxeye (Caja-vras) *Leucanthemum vulgare,* p, E
Dandelion, *Taraxacum officinale agg.,* p, M, P
  Dandelion, *Taraxacum spectabile,* p, E
Dead-nettle, Red, *Lamium purpureum,* a, P
Dock, Broad leaved (Tavol) *Rumex obtusifolius,* p, M/B, D
Dock, Curled, *Rumex crispus,* p D
  Dock, Fiddle (Tavol) *Rumex pulcher,* p, P
Evening Primrose, *Oenothera lamarckiana,* b, E
Evening Primrose, Small-flowered. *Oenothera sp.,* b, E
Fat Hen, *Chenopodium album* a, D
Fluellen, Sharp-leaved, *Kickxia elatine,* a, E
Forget-me-not, Changing, *Mysotis discolor,* a, E
Forget-me-not, Field, *Myosotis arvensis,* a, E
Foxglove (Manek lowarn) *Digitalis purpurea,* b, M, E
Fumitory, Common, *Fumaria officinalis,* a, E
Fumitory, Common Ramping, *Fumaria muralis ssp. boraei,* a, E
Fumitory, Tall Ramping, *Fumaria bastardii,* a, E
Gorse (Eythynen-Frynk) *Ulex europaeus,* p, M/B, W
Groundsel, *Senecio vulgaris,* a, W
Hawk's-beard, Smooth, *Crepis capillaris,* a, P
Hawkweed, Umbellate, *Hieracium umbellatum,* p, E
  Hemlock (Kegysen) *Conium maculatum,* b, E
Herb-Robert, *Geranium robertianum,* a, E
Hogweed (Panesen) *Heracleum sphondylium,* p, M, W
Knapweed, Black, *Centaurea nigra,* p, E
Knotgrass, *Polygonum aviculare,* a, M, W
  Knotgrass sp., *Polygonum arenastrum,* a, W

PLANT SPECIES IN FIELDS

Mayweed, Scented, *Chamomela recutica*, a E
Mayweed, Scentless, *Tripleurospermum inodorum*, a, M, W
Mouse-ear, Common, *Cerastium fontanum glabrescens*, a, P
Mouse-ear, Sticky, *Cerastium glomeratum*, a, P
Mustard, Black (Kedhow) *Brassica nigra, a*, W
Mustard, Hedge (Kedhow) *Sisymbrium officinale*, a, M, D
Nettle, Common (Lynasen) *Urtica dioica*, p, M/B, W
 Nettle, Small, *Urtica urens*, a, E
Nightshade, Black (Morel) *Solanum nigrum*, a, W
Nipplewort, *Lapsana communis*, a, P
 Orache, Common, *Atriplex patula*, a, M, D
 Ox-tongue, Bristly, *Picris echioides*, a/b, E
Pansy, Field, *Viola arvensis*, a, E
 Pansy, hybrid, *Viola arvensis x tricolor*, a, E
Parsley, Cow (Persyl) *Anthriscus sylvestris*, p, W
Parsley, Fool's (Persyl) *Aethusa cynapium*, a, E
 Parsley Piert (Persyl) *Aphanes arvensis*, a, E
 Pearlwort, Procumbent, *Sagina procumbens*, p, P
 Persicaria, *Polygonum nodosum*, a, E
 Persicaria, Pale, *Persicaria lapathifolia*, a, W
Pimpernel, Scarlet, *Anagallis arvensis*, a, E
Pineapple Weed, *Matricaria discoidea*, a, P
Plantain, Greater (Ladan-les) *Plantago major*, p, M, P
Plantain, Ribwort, *Plantago lanceolata*, p, W
 Poppy, Common, *Papaver rhoeas*, a, W
Ragwort (Madere-bras) *Senecio jacobaea*, p, M, P
 Rape, *Brassica napus*, a, D
Redshank, *Persicaria maculosa*, a, W
 Rush, Toad, *Juncus bufonius*, a
Scabious, Sheep's-bit (Pen-glas) *Jasione montana*, p, M, E
Self-heal, *Prunella vulgaris*, p, E
 Shepherd's Purse, *Capsella bursa-pastoris*, a, P
 Snapdragon, Lesser, *Misopates orontium*, a, E
Sorrel, Common (Tavolen-wherow) *Rumex acetosa*, p, W
 Sow-thistle, Field, *Sonchus arvensis*, p, E
Sow-thistle, Prickly, *Sonchus asper*, a or b, P
Sow-thistle, Smooth, *Sonchus oleraceus*, a or b, P
 Spearwort, Lesser, *Ranunculus flammula*, p, E
Speedwell, Common Field, *Veronica persica*, a, E

PLANT SPECIES IN FIELDS

Speedwell, Germander, *Veronica chamaedrys*, p, E
Speedwell, Thyme-leaved, *Veronica serpyllifolia*, p, E
  Speedwell, Wall, *Veronica arvensis*, a, E
  Spurge, Sun (Flamgos) *Euphorbia helioscopia*, a, W
  Spurrey, Corn, *Spergula arvensis*, a, M/B, E
  St John's Wort, Trailing, *Hypericum humifusum*, p, E
Strawberry, Wild, *Fragaria vesca*, p, E
  Swine-cress, *Coronopus squamatus*, a, D
  Swine-cress, Lesser, *Coronopus didymus*, a, D
  Tare, Hairy, *Vicia hirsuta* a, E
Thistle, Creeping, *Cirsium arvense*, p, M, W
  Thistle, Marsh, *Cirsium palustre*, b, M, E
  Thistle, Musk, *Carduus nutans*, b, E
Thistle, Spear, *Cirsium vulgare*, p, P
Trefoil, Greater Bird's-foot (Mullyon-melen) *Lotus pedunculatus*, p, M, E
  Trefoil, Hop (Tyrdelen) *Trifolium campestre* a, E
  Trefoil, Lesser Yellow (Tyrdelen) *Trifolium dubium*, a, E
  Turnip, Wild, *Brassica rapa*, b, W
Vetch, Narrow-leaved (Gwek) *Vicia sativa ssp.nigra*, a, E
Vetch, Tufted (Gwek) *Vicia cracca*, p, E
Vetchling, Meadow, *Lathyrus pratensis*, p, E
  Watercress, Fool's, *Apium nodiflorum*, p, E
  Willowherb, American, *Epilobium ciliatum*, p, P
Willow-herb, Broad-leaved, *Epilobium montanum*, p, M, W
  Willowherb, Great, *Epilobium hirsutum*, p, E
  Willowherb, Hoary, *Epilobium parviflorum*, p M, E
  Willowherb hybrid, *Epilobium ciliatum x parviflorum*, p, E
  Woundwort, Field, *Stachys arvensis*, a, E
Woundwort, Hedge, *Stachys sylvatica*, p, E
Woundwort, Marsh, *Stachys palustris*, p, E
Yarrow, *Achillea millifolium*, p, E

GRASSES IN FIELDS (Not included in hedge survey)

Barley, *Hordeum distichum,* a
Bent, Black, *Agrostis gigantea,* p
Bent, Brown, *Agrostis canina,* p
Bent, Common, *Agrostis capillaris,* p
Bent, Creeping, *Agrostis stolonifera,* p
Brome, Meadow, *Bromus commutatus,* a/b
Brome, Slender Soft, *Bromus lepidus,* a/b
Brome, Soft, *Bromus hordeaceus,* a/b
Cock's-foot, *Dactylis glomerata,* p, B
Couch, Common (Stroil) *Elytrigia repens,* p
Dog's-tail, Crested, *Cynosurus cristatus,* p
Fescue, Meadow, *Festuca pratensis,* p
Fescue, Squirel-tail, *Vulpia bromoides,* a
Foxtail, Marsh, *Alopecurus geniculatus,* p
Foxtail, Meadow, *Alopecurus pratensis,* p
Grass, Sweet Vernal, *Anthoxanthum oderatum,* p
Hair-grass, Tufted, *Deschampsia caespitosa,* p
Meadow-grass, Annual, *Poa annua,* a, B
Meadow-grass, Rough, *Poa trivialis,* p
Meadow-grass, Smooth, *Poa pratensis,* p
Oat, Wild, *Avena fatua,* a
Oat-grass, False, *Arrhenatherum elatius var. bulbosum,* a
Ryegrass (Yvre) *Lolium perenne,* p
Ryegrass, Italian, *Lolium multiflorum,* a/b
Soft-grass, Creeping, *Holcus mollis,* p
Timothy, *Phleum pratense,* p, B
Wheat, *Triticum aestivum,* a
Yorkshire Fog, *Holcus lanatus,* p, B

With thanks to R.J.Murphy for confirming a number of identifications and to J.S.Fortescue for help with locating species.

Appendix D

THE 13 SPECIES OF BUTTERFLIES ASSOCIATED WITH HEDGES IN CORNWALL (Spalding, pers. comm.). (* species with very close association with hedges)

Name	Hedge needs of Caterpillars	Of Adult
Comma	Nettle	Tall sheltered hedges, Bramble
* Gatekeeper	Sheltered with Grasses:	Tall hedges with Bramble
Green Hairstreak	Broom/Gorse	Tall hedges, Broom & Gorse
Holly Blue	Ivy/Holly	Tall hedges with Ivy/Holly
Large Skipper	Sheltered with Grasses:	Sheltered grassy banks
Meadow Brown	Coarse Grasses	Grassy banks and hedges
* Orange Tip	Shaded, Hedge Garlic:	Shady with Hedge Garlic
Red Admiral	Nettle	Sunny with Nettle
* Ringlet	Damp & shady grassy banks:	Grassy banks & hedges
Silver-washed Fritillary	Shady with Violets	Tall hedges & Bramble
Small Copper	Sorrel on banks	Open hedges with Sorrel
Small Skipper	Yorkshire Fog on banks/verges:	Grassy banks/hedges
Small Tortoiseshell	Nettle	Sunny banks with Nettle
Speckled Wood	Tall with Grasses in shade:	Tall & shady with Bramble

Appendix E

LIST OF LARGER MOTHS ASSOCIATED WITH HEDGES IN CORNWALL.

The following list of 150 larger moths (macro-moths) are those that in A. Spalding's opinion are most closely associated with hedges in Cornwall. Some of the species are widespread and may be found in many other different kinds of habitat. The 12 species with an especially close association with hedgerows are shewn*. The list only includes species which are self-sustaining in the wide range of Cornish hedgerow habitats.

1. Macro-moths associated with shrubs or trees in hedges (n=76).

Barred Yellow, *Cidaria fulvata*
Blue-bordered Carpet, *Plemyria rubiginata*
Brimstone Moth, *Opisthograptis luteolata*
Buff Arches, *Habrosyne pyritoides*
Canary-shouldered Thorn, *Ennomos alniaria*
Centre-barred Sallow, *Atethmia centrago*
Chinese Character, *Cilix glaucata*
Clouded Border, *Lomaspilis marginata*
Clouded Drab, *Orthosia incerta*
Clouded Silver, *Lomographa temerata*
Common Emerald, *Hemithea aestivaria*
Common Lutestring, *Ochropacha duplaris*
Common Marbled Carpet,
    Chloroclysta truncata
Common Quaker, *Orthosia cerasi*
Common White Wave, *Cabera pusaria*
Copper Underwing, *Amphipyra pyramidea*
Coxcomb Prominent, *Ptilodon capucina*
Dark Marbled Carpet, *Chloroclysta citrata*
December Moth, *Poecilocampa populi*
Dotted Border, *Agriopis marginaria*
Early Grey, *Xylocampa areola*
Early Moth, *Theria primaria*
Early Thorn, *Selenia dentaria*
Early Tooth-striped, *Trichopteryx carpinata*
Emperor Moth, *Saturnia pavonia*
Feathered Thorn, *Colotois pennaria*
Flounced Chestnut, *Agrochola helvola*
Fox Moth, *Macrothylacia rubi*
Grass Emerald, *Pseudoterpna pruinata*
Green Pug, *Chloroclystis rectangulata*
Green-brindled Crescent,
    Allophyes oxyacanthae
Grey Dagger, *Acronnicta psi*
* Haworth's Pug, *Eupithecia haworthiata*
Hebrew Character, *Orthosia gothica*
Iron Prominent, *Notodonta dromedarius*
Large Emerald, *Geometra papilionaria*
Least Black Arches, *Nola confusalis*
Lesser Swallow Prominent, *Pheosia gnoma*
Light Emerald, *Campaea margaritata*
Lilac Beauty, *Apeira syringaria*
Little Emerald, *Jodis lactearia*
March Moth, *Alsophila aescularia*
Merveille du Jour, *Dichonia aprilina*
Mottled Pug, *Eupithecia exiguata*
Mottled Umber, *Erannis defoliaria*
Nut-tree Tussock, *Colocasia coryli*
Oak-tree Pug, *Eupithecia dodoneata*
Peach Blossom, *Thyatira batis*
Pebble Hook-tip, *Drepana falcataria*
Pebble Prominent, *Eligmodonta ziczac*
Peppered Moth, *Biston betularia*
* Pretty Chalk Carpet, *Melanthia procellata*
Purple Thorn, *Selenia tetralunaria*
Scalloped Hazel, *Odontopera bidentata*
Scalloped Hook-tip, *Falcaria lacertinaria*
Scalloped Oak, *Crocallis elinguaria*
Scorched Carpet, *Ligdia adustata*
Sharp-angled Peacock, *Semiothisa alternaria*
Small Anglesbades, *Euplexia lucipara*
* Small Emerald, *Hemistola chrysoprasaria*
Small Fanfoot, *Herminia grisealis*
Small Quaker, *Orthosia cruda*
Swallow Prominent, *Pheosia tremula*
Swallow-tailed Moth, *Ourapteryx sambucaria*
The Brick, *Agrochola circellaris*
The Chestnut, *Conistra vaccinii*
The Dun-bar, *Cosmia trapezina*

MOTHS IN CORNISH HEDGES

* The Fern, *Horisme tersata*
The Lackey, *Malacosoma neustria*
Twin-spotted Quaker, *Orthosia munda*
White-pinion, *Lomographa bimaculata*
Willow Beauty, *Peribatodes rhomboidaria*
Winter Moth, *Operophtera brumata*
Yellow Horned, *Achyla flavicornis*
Yellow-barred Brindle, *Acasis viretata*
Yellow-line Quaker, *Agrochola macilenta*

2. Macro-moths associated with ground-layer plants in hedges (n=56).

Barred Straw, *Eulithis pyraliata*
Beaded Chestnut, *Agrochola lychnides*
Blood-vein, *Timandra griseata*
Buff Ermine, *Spilosoma luteum*
Burnished Brass, *Diachrysia chrysitis*
Chimney Sweeper, *Odezia atrata*
Cloaked Carpet, *Euphyia biangulata*
Common Carpet, *Epirrhoe alternata*
Common Rustic, *Mesapamea secalis*
Cream Wave, *Scopula floslactata*
* Crewe Jasione Pug, *Epirrhoe denota jasioneata*
Dark Arches, *Apamea monoglypha*
Dark-barred Twin-spot Carpet, *Xanthorhoe ferrugata*
Double-striped Pug, *Gymnoscelis rufifasciata*
Flame Carpet, *Xanthorhoe designata*
Flounced Rustic, *Luperina testacea*
Frosted Orange, *Gortyna flavago*
Garden Carpet, *Xanthorhoe fluctuata*
Green Arches, *Anaplectoides prasina*
Knot Grass, *Acronicta rumicis*
Lime-speck Pug, *Epirrhoe centaureata*
Marbled Minor, *Oligia strigilis*
Marbled White Spot, *Protodeltote pygarga*
Mullein Wave, *Scopula marginepunctata*
Muslin Moth, *Diaphora mendica*
Pale Mottled Willow, *Caradrina clavipalpis*
Purple Bar, *Cosmorhoe ocellata*
Red Twin-spot Carpet, *Xanthorhoe spaticearia*
Riband Wave, *Idaea aversata*
Rosy Minor, *Mesoliqia literosa*
Royal Mantle, *Catarhoe cuculata*
Ruddy Carpet, *Catarhoe rubidata*
Rufous Minor, *Oligia versicolor*

Sandy Carpet, *Perizoma flavofasciata*
Sharp-angled Carpet, *Epirrhoe unangulata*
* Shoulder Stripe, *Anticlea badiata*
Silver-ground Carpet, *Xanthorhoe montanata*
* Small Fan-footed Wave, *Idaea biselata*
Small Phoenix, *Ecliptopera silaceata*
Small Rivulet, *Perizoma alchemillata*
Speckled Yellow, *Pseudopanthera macularia*
Tawny Marbled Minor, *Oligia latruncula*
The Lychnis, *Hadena bicruris*
The Rivulet, *Perizoma affinitata*
The Rustic, *Hoplodrina blanda*
The Snout, *Hypena proboscidalis*
The Spectacle, *Abrostola triplasia*
* The Streamer, *Abrostola derivata*
The Uncertain, *Hoplodrina alsines*
Treble Lines, *Charanyca trigrammica*
Valerian Pug, *Eupithecia valerianata*
Water Carpet, *Lampropteryx suffumata*
White Ermine, *Spilosoma lubricipeda*
White-spotted Pug, *Epirrhoe tripunctaria*
Wood Carpet, *Epirrhoe rivata*
Yellow Shell, *Camptogramma bilineata*

3. Macro-moths associated with both ground-layer plants and shrubs/trees in hedges in Cornwall (n=18).

Angle Shades, *Phlogophora meticulosa*
Beautiful Golden Y, *Autographa pulchrina*
Broad-bordered Yellow Underwing, *Noctua fimbriata*
Common Pug, *Eupithecia vulgata*
Double Square-spot, *Xestia triangulum*
Grey Arches, *Polia nebulosa*
Grey Pug, *Eupithecia subfuscata*
Ingrailed Clay, *Diarsia mendica*
Large Yellow Underwing, *Noctua pronuba*
Lesser Broad-bordered Yellow Underwing, *Noctua janthina*
Lesser Yellow Underwing, *Noctua comes*
Plain Golden Y, *Autographa jota*
Purple Clay, *Diarsia brunnea*
* Small Blood-vein, *Scopula imitaria*
The Fan-foot, *Herminia tarsipennalis*
The Magpie, *Abraxas grossulariata*
The Vapourer, *Orgyia antiqua*
The V-Pug, *Chloroclystis v-ata*

MOTHS IN CORNISH HEDGES

4. Macro-moths with a close association with lichens on walls and hedges in Cornwall.

Marbled Beauty, *Cryphia domestica*   Marbled Green, *Cryphia muralis*

Appendix F

NUMBERS OF PLANT AND ANIMAL CATAGORIES ASSOCIATED WITH THE OAK IN GREAT BRITAIN (from Whitlock, 1985).

Mammals	32
Birds	68
Butterfly (feeding on leaves)	1
Butterflies (associated)	36
Moths (feeding on leaves)	23
Moth (feeding on dead leaves)	1
Moths (feeding on lichens)	8
Moth (feeding on bark)	1
Micro-moths (feeding on oak)	6
Other micro-moths	21
Beetles	44
Spiders	21
Bees, Wasps & Ants	13
Plant Bugs (feeding on oak)	28
Other Plant Bugs	15
Associated plants	174
Ferns	10
Some Lichens	31

TOTAL: 533 Species

Wildlife over-wintering in Cornish hedges is sheltered by the multi-layered growth of traditional hedge management. Close-trimming removes the natural protection against cold easterly winds which kill vulnerable plants and animals. As elsewhere in Britain, the snow itself causes little damage even in Cornwall.

Printed by Rowe the Printers, Hayle. Tel: (0736) 756435